Altar of the Earth

Altar of the Earth
The Life, Land and Spirit of Tibet

Peter Gold

Snow Lion Publications
Ithaca, New York USA

Snow Lion Publications
P.O. Box 6483
Ithaca, New York 14851
USA

Library of Congress Cataloging-in-Publication Data

Gold, Peter.
    Altar of the earth.

    1. Tibet (China)—Description and travel.
2. Gold, Peter—Journeys—China—Tibet.   I. Title.
DS786.G63   1987   915.1'50458   87-12941
ISBN 0-937938-44-0

Contents

"Kind wings of the windhorse
show compassion in this vast land;
oh my beautiful one!
When I see the wings of the windhorse
I remember how vast the earth is,
and how far my journey
and how I wish I could use your wings."

—*from an old Lhasa folksong*

To the idea and reality that is Tibet

Acknowledgements

My gratitude to the people of Tibet whose hospitality and kind help were essential to realizing this book. Also special thanks to Keven Cassidy, Nate Cutler, Keith Dowman, John Hammer, Arlene Olson, Sheldon Robinson, Yeshe Sonam and my editor, Christine Cox, for their advice and aid.

To the Altar

Abode of the Gods. Shangri La. "Because it's there." The world has long nurtured a consuming fascination for the land, and the ways of life and spirit of the Tibetan people.

Quite likely, no other living culture has so fired the imaginations of millions. The flames have been fed by Tibet's physical isolation and unbroken ties to an ancient past, as well as by our own psychic hunger for a Paradise Lost and new worlds to explore.

Over the centuries, Westerners could only speculate about the beautiful but forbidding landscape of the Tibetan Plateau and that culture which had fostered one of humanity's most sophisticated spiritual systems. And only in recent years, in fact, have we begun to get accurate answers to our questions.

Tibet is the last in a long line of "untouched" indigenous civilizations, having unbroken roots dating to the dawn of humankind. These cultures contributed timeless ideas, ways of expression and material achievements that continue to be held in high regard. But, unlike our contemporary "adolescent" cultures, theirs were generally in compassionate balance with their world, and within themselves.

Tibetans had created such a way of life, over the centuries, one predicated upon the spiritual view rather than upon material gain. By surviving far longer than its contemporaries, Tibet has saved this ancient legacy for us all.

What specifically was preserved in that fabled land which one might call the Altar of the Earth?

I believe it's the awareness that an entire nation can set aside non-essential physical needs and rigid attitudes to embark upon the spiritual path through life. Can the West, like the early Tibetans, eventually succeed in reorienting its genius toward alleviating self-created suffering and the realization of its people's ultimate enlightenment?

Most cultures speak of an earlier, golden age. I believe them. Centuries ago there was space enough to easily nurture peaceful, spiritual civilizations. The greater the physical -and psychic-space, the less the chance of violence befalling them.

Tibet's land certainly provides the necessary space, as well as a stimulating environment for maintaining an inspired state of mind. The breathtaking vistas, the ever-changing weather, the total interplay of earth, water, sun's fire and air compose an alchemical brew which readily distills into the etheric element of the enlightened mind.

Add to their environmental inspiration the transcendent science of consciousness, brought by early Indian Buddhist teachers, and one can appreciate that special elixir of life which has been preserved atop the Altar of the Earth for all who seek harmony and peace, without and within.

It all began almost thirteen hundred years ago and almost ended during the past thirty. Although Tibet was able to survive into our era, due to its previously impenetrable location, in 1959 it finally succumbed to the overwhelming material might of the modern world. The drastic changes witnessed in Tibet over the past generation are vivid reminders of that duality which Buddhism and the natural way of living teach us to avoid.

Yet, while the old complexion of life appears to be gone forever, the spirit of Tibet seems to have prevailed. Like deeply buried seeds that are incubated by a forest fire and sprout to renew the trees, so too with the ageless message of Tibetan civilization. Lamas and other gifted Tibetan teachers now travel the world over, imparting perennial ideas and values that had been transmitted to them, in a similar manner, down through the ages.

What is it about their land, way of life, and quality of mind and spirit that they have congealed into the phenomenon called Tibet?

Let's explore it together on our journey to the Altar of the Earth.

BEGINNINGS
THE YARLUNG VALLEY

"A golden house, a good house,
with a turquouise floor
and golden stairs;
let us have the blessings on the turquoise floor.
On the turquoise floor lie sacred barley kernels,
and when I toss them into the air
all my wishes will come true."

—*from an old* chang *drinking song*

Origins

Beginnings

"Up there, just below the summit of holy Mount Kongpori, that's where our father lived," explained the old man, wearing a silk brocade hat, big turquoise earring and a homespun woolen cloak.

He was illustrating his story by pointing significantly, with one hand, to the receding summit of the arid peak that towers over the town of Tsetang. While with the other, he held on for dear life, as our tractor bounced mercilessly over rocks and through creeks on its way into town.

The old folks, of course, know the "truth" about the origin of the Tibetan people, that they come from the unusual marital union of a saintly monkey and a fierce mountain divinity who lived together in a cave atop Mount Kongpori.

Sitting here, now, in the shelter of a rocky overhang part way up the sacred mountain, I can just begin to make out the array of prayer flags at its summit, placed there by the present-day children of these divine beings.

Someday I'll climb all the way up it. But today, the wind's too strong and, besides, there's something magical and mysterious about looking up at the huge rocky dome, then climbing it with the mind.

Tibetans explain that Chenrezi, bodhisattva of compassion and savior of beings in the six realms of illusory existence, had emanated here into a life form more compatible with the earthly plane of existence. Since, in those days, there were no beings that could be described as human, he took the form of a benevolent monkey.

The monkey saint lived a quiet and inspired life in his mountain cave. It had a superb view of the wide Yarlung Tsangpo River Valley, its pastel peaks and white clouds set into a lapis blue sky.

At around this time another enlightened being incarnated in terrestrial form. Drolma, the Great Goddess, took a form equally well adapted to the caves and heights of Kongpori. She transformed herself into an alluring but fierce spirit of the rocky crags.

Her arrival meant an end to the monkey saint's solitude. For a long while (were they days or centuries?) he would be roused from his meditations by incessant sobbing coming from the ''rock demoness''' cave.

"Oh monkey, I'm so lonely. Why don't we live together and have a family?" she cried.

"An impossible idea!" were his first thoughts. But in his infinite compassion and wisdom he quickly realized that this would be a beneficial thing to do.

So, from out of the union of two very different yet similar beings came the Tibetan people.

Today's Tibetans, in fact, see themselves as newly tamed wild people: wild as a monkey can act wildly; wild as the physical qualities of their high, rocky land; wild as the unbridled mind which they, as an entire civilization, have embarked upon taming.

And they also see themselves as among the most fortunate beings on earth because of their access to the Buddhist teachings, which are taming their mental wildness. Every Tibetan knows that in historical times these teachings have been transmitted unbroken to them by lamas and saintly teachers whom they consider to be emanations of enlightened beings.

But one suspects that the older Tibetans, particularly, believe that the Buddhist path was somatically instilled within them, from the earliest times, by the monkey-Chenrezi and the wild mountain divinity-Drolma.

In the end, I believe that this was what the old man was trying to tell me.

The First Field of Tibet

When the monkey incarnation of Chenrezi slept with a demoness of the rocky crags in a cave high atop Mount Kongpori, they conceived six children. Each went on to found one of the six original tribes of the Tibetan People.

As children, they would scamper down from the high cave to the broad valley below it. They would play in the trees and grasslands and swim in the massive river that coursed past snow-capped peaks. This was a favored place too for their father, the divine monkey being. For it was in this area that he chose to plant his first field of barley. He worked the First Field in this beautiful and magical land, to provide for the needs of his descendants until they too could jump the wheel of continuous death and rebirth and attain the buddhas' realm. His children loved the field so much that they used it daily as their *tsetang*, their playground or "playing field."

Generations later, descendants of the first people of Tibet would create a town in view of Kongpori Mountain and call it Tsetang.

Right now, I am sitting in the middle of what may be the very field to have been planted by the monkey emanation of Chenrezi. And from here one can appreciate the perfectness of the setting.

The Yarlung Tsangpo, highest major river system in the world, must have flooded this plain along a broad bend in its path innumerable times down through the ages, depositing countless layers of rich soil.

A cache of gray earth, full of the mineral distillate of the highest mountains on earth, was left after the waters had receded. When the people began to farm here, they helped the river renew the fields and nurture the crops by digging irrigation channels into the fertile soil. In time it became one of the most prolific agricultural regions in Tibet. In fact, oral legend aside, the Yarlung Valley—at whose head sits Tsetang—is indeed the area where Tibetan agriculture seems to have begun.

Legacy of the all-compassionate Chenrezi or just down to earth common sense? Regardless of its origins, agriculture has contributed to the Yarlung Valley's becoming known as the "Cradle of Tibetan Civilization."

At the head of the cradle sits Kongpori Mountain, the Yarlung Tsangpo River and possibly the first field. At the other end looms the valley's sacred mountain Yarlha Shampo. The Yarlung Valley splits in two, just south of Tsetang, and within these quiet precincts the first major dynasty of Tibetan kings flourished, setting a pattern that was to be followed for centuries.

A few kilometers south of Tsetang the Thepu dynasty left the Yumbulhakhang, the Mother's Child's God's House, said to have been (before its recent destruction and reconstruction) the oldest building in Tibet. Legend has it that Yumbulhakhang was built by the first supernatural king, Nyatri Tsenpo. He had descended, it relates, from the sky realm to the summit of a sacred peak named Lhababri, along a" skyladder" filament in the form of a rainbow-like cord emanating from the crown of his head.

Nyatri Tsenpo was the first of the first line of Tibetan kings who were not mortals, but "Sons of the Sky"; *mu* cord-ladders would also serve to retract their bodies after death, their bodies dissolving—according to pre-Buddhist, Bon texts— into rainbow light as they rose into the sky.

Thus, the first field, the first Tibetan people, the first building and the first dynasty of kings had all arisen among these quiet, fertile fields.

Many firsts. The rest is history.

The Kings

The Rainbow Path from the Sky

Way up, in one of the highest rooms of the Yumbulhakhang, atop a high hill in a high valley, it can be found. It is there, amid silk banners, elaborate altars and carved pillars: a color-fully painted wall mural. And depicted on it, an event of singular importance to the Tibetan people.

It tells the tale of an ancient king who reigned so long ago that his personal qualities and deeds are now recalled only through the filter of myth.

Nyatri Tsenpo was the first in a long line of *chögyal*, religious kings. They ruled with an iron sword, wielding it against human adversaries such as their neighbors the Chinese, whom Srongtsen Gampo, the most illustrious of the *chögyal*, had succeeded in conquering.

But they also wielded a fiery sword of a diamond hard material. It cut through the dark ignorance of those self-generated impediments to enlightenment that kept their people in true bondage: those shrouded, noisy, unwholesome thoughts and emotions of the mind.

The mural shows Nyatri Tsenpo, having just manifest from the sky, sitting below the summit of the sacred mountain, Lhababri. Later, according to the painting, he arrives at this very spot where he builds this castle from which to rule his kingdom.

Another section depicts more subtle metaphysical qualities of his being. The ancient annals say that when his body came out of the sky, it emanated spontaneously out of a *mu* cord. Rather than showing his body, in this section he is symbolically depicted as a *pecha*, a sacred book, entering the high tower at the end of a rainbow. The *pecha* contains the teachings of Buddhism whose tenets, legend has it, he instituted on the Altar of the Earth.

Symbolically speaking, the *pecha* text embodies the spiritual voices of Nyatri Tsenpo and the subsequent religious kings of Tibet. Similarly, the eyes now begin to view this building as much more than a castle and an icon of ancient Tibetan royalty. It can be seen to manifest, in its tower-like architecture, the power of the word: the voice of the Buddhist teachings which, like the blue sky, is infinite, blemishless, a bright and seamless unity.

As such, Yumbulhakhang is a lighthouse, sending out its noble beams of enlightenment for all of us, who are sailors on the ocean of the Great Void, to see, remember and become.

Valley of the Kings

For centuries, the supernatural kings would come and go by way of the sky until one, named Drigum (Slain by Pollution), managed to sever his *mu* cord with his own sword during battle obscured by clouds of ashes.

After Drigum's fateful accident the kings of Yarlung had to be born and die on the earth, and their bodies disposed of in an appropriate manner when the *namshe*, the consciousness, departed from them.

From his royal lineage in the Yarlung Valley came some of the most revered kings in the annals of Tibetan religion.

The glory of that ancient period focuses on this eroding earthen hillock, and several other such manmade platforms, here at the village of Chongye, in the Valley of the Kings.

Atop this vaguely four-sided mound stands a modest temple. Its modesty, though, is one only of size. This is understandable considering the small area it is able to occupy, as well as the difficult economic realities behind its reconstruction in 1983.

Welcome to the temple and tomb of the illustrious seventh century *chögyal*, the Religious King Songtsen Gampo. His *durkhang*, "bone house" tumulus stands at the base of a mountain slope, within a valley dotted by many other such earthen mounds.

The antiquity of this burial practice goes back well beyond that of today's "sky burials." wherein bodies are filleted and bones crushed for the pleasure of birds of prey.

In ancient Tibet, the burial monuments were meant as a symbol—to all who would walk the later road of life—of their ancestors' deeds and times, and to make the entombed king, queen or important person appear "larger than life."

During the heyday of Central Tibetan nobility, the royal necropolis at Chongye was the main site of their entombment. Even after Songtsen Gampo moved his dynasty to a pleasant valley to the northwest, which he called Lhasa, Chongye continued to be the final resting place of the kings.

The practice of enshrining illustrious persons began to change as the centuries passed. Lamas became the focus of the people's reverence. Lamas are considered earthly embodiments of the mental energies of enlightened beings—buddhas and bodhisattvas—and serve as the primary spiritual teachers to the people on their winding roads toward enlightenment. As such they have become even more important to Tibetans than were their kings. To show their respect and preserve some of the lama's physically-generated spiritual power, the people had begun to entomb their revered lamas in stone or sometimes jewel-studded, golden *chörtens*.

Chörtens are decidedly vertical structures, even more so than the kings' tombs. They have a variety of esoteric meanings relating to the alchemical elements, cardinal directions, the tantric lineages and the ideas and procedures utilized in the evolution of the consciousness toward enlightenment. In essence, they are symbols of the sky-like infinity of the awakened mind.

The presence of the lamas' preserved remains within them, makes *chörtens*—like the earthy tombs of the ancient deified kings—more than mere mausoleums.

They are symbols of a spiritual path through life. They are beacons to a blissful future, founded on a past that continues in the legends, memories and ways of living of those who make the pilgrimage to the Valley of the Kings.

The Old and the New

"Chandruk *gompa* is the oldest monastery in Tibet," one of its monks proudly informed me. "It's one thousand three hundred and thirty-two years old!"

"It was built by the great *dharma* king, Songtsen Gampo. Four generations of kings would pass before the monastery at Samye was established farther west, along the Yarlung Tsangpo river."

His point was well taken, since we are often informed that Samye *gompa* is the oldest monastery in Tibet. Well, there is a certain degree of truth to both assertions, in that as far as major monastic establishments go, Samye is still the oldest, since that at Chandruk village is more a temple than a monastery.

In a sense it is an esoteric, spiritual luxury that the Yarlung Tibetans can participate in a good-natured debate over which of their holy places is the older, when both are well over one thousand years in age! For Tibetans, however, the difference remains of great importance, long after we've stopped counting.

Old things are the foundation of Tibetans' lives and the basis of the new. For Westerners, on the contrary, old things are the basis of the romantic but are, otherwise, the bane of the

new. Still, somewhere within the vacancy of our individual
and social lives—the inevitable result in a society whose eyes
are permanently focused toward the future—there is that insinuating recognition that something precious has been lost.

So we journey to places like Tibet to regain the wisdom of
the past. Even a brief stay in Tibet indelibly imprints upon
the mind the fact that for its people the present *is* the past,
Chinese soldiers and Western tourists notwithstanding.

Here we are, at the oldest temple in Tibet, standing before
the ancient statues of its founders, the great seventh century
king Songtsen Gampo and his two queens from Nepal and
China.

Here we are, in Chandruk village, as old as the original,
crumbling masonry and weather-worn beams of the temple.
Probably older.

Life continues much the same today as it has for a millen-
nium. Three generations, perhaps four, of women and girls
sit and spin their sheep's wool, nurse their infants, thresh and
winnow ears of barley recently harvested from their fields. All
are dressed the same, in black, homespun woolen *chubas*,
brightly colored striped aprons and a touch of turquoise or
coral around their necks and in their ears. They live, dress,
act and, in most essential respects, think as they did over a
thousand years ago when the temple was built.

Here we are, watching the villagers rebuild Chandruk temple in the same old style in which it was designed and built
by their ancestors. This must be a momentous time for the
village people and temple's monks, having found the necessary resources and political climate for the first time since 1964,
when it was all but destroyed during the horrors of the cultural revolution.

And here we are, having just walked seven kilometers from
an equally significant restoration. There, we had climbed up
to Yumbulhakhang, ancestral home of the Yarlung kings. It
is considered by legend to be over two thousand years old. In
reality though it probably was erected "only" one thousand
four hundred years ago! Yumbulhakhang too was destroyed

during the reign of terror and has been rebuilt, in the ancient style, during the past three years.

What is significant to my mind in all of this, is the Tibetan drive for continuity. At the basis of the Tibetan way of perceiving reality is the people's belief in the cyclic nature of phenomena and time. One's consciousness, in its pilgrimage through the eons, takes an infinite number of rebirths until gaining the necessary clarity and freedom from the impediments of self-created obstacles to attain enlightenment. This is symbolized as a huge wheel in the clutches of Yama, God of Death.

Likewise, time is conceived of cyclically, rather than as a line leading forever away from a dead past into an uncertain future, as in our way of thinking. Tibetans recognize cycles of various lengths in the natural cosmos, from incredibly long "world eons" to convenient sixty year cycles reckoned by a combination of twelve animals and five elements.

For Tibetans, all in the phenomenal world are an expression of the cycles of time. Old is not only old; it's also new, and now. The corollary also holds true. When Tibetans look to the future, their inspiration is necessarily from the past.

Perhaps their firm foundation in ancient ways will prove the needed source of their strength in meeting the uncertain times of change yet to come.

Land

Silence, Solace and Solitude

All over the world and throughout the ages, those who have sought solace would seek out silence and solitude.

And silence and solitude is what Tibet is all about.

Take this country lane in the Yarlung Valley. It's a long way to anywhere from here, and a most pleasurable way of getting there.

High arid hills (in Tibet the "hills" touch heaven) define the broad, irrigated green valley which is the cradle of Tibetan agriculture and its civilization.

The lane winds its way through numerous tiny villages that seem to have grown from out of the very earth. Their stone and adobe walls are miniature expressions of the mountain ridges above them while their people's smiling and inquisitive faces shine in the sunlight like the barley and rape seed crowding their fields.

Despite an intensely hot sun the breeze cools one, bringing subtle smells and sounds along with its relief. Only a periodic bird, bee or fly breaks the overall silence. The silence is so pervasive that even when the rain does manage to fall over this otherwise desert landscape, the tiny drops impart hardly a sound (or a stain for that matter) to the valley floor.

Here and there the narrow lane passes through groves of poplars, stands of willows and periodic clumps of hemp, tall as trees. And it soon merges into nothingness at a gap in a stone and earthen wall. Beyond it spread barley fields with their muddy irrigation channels. Beyond them, dry earth, lonely shrubs and purple wildflowers are everywhere, revealing the true identity of the land.

The occasional bleat of a sheep, bang of its bell, and a snatch of song by a villager harvesting her field, are all that one can hear.

Otherwise, silence.

Silence, like an infinity view down the spreading valley.

Silence, like the clouds gathering momentarily above it.

Silence, like the sandy gullies that turn into boiling torrents when the heavy rains do eventually come.

Silence, like the narrow lane curling around one mountain's base then the next.

Silence, like the wildflowers subtly swaying to the touch of an unseen breeze.

Silence, golden like the sun now beginning to flood the landscape with warmth, bringing life wherever it goes.

Silence, in solitude, brings one great solace, atop the Altar of the Earth.

Samye

At the Crossroads

"Is there a god still living up there?"

"*Ta pepsong; Lha haiborii toghola mindu.*"

So came the answer from several monks and villagers living around Samye Monastery, whom I'd queried about the prominent hill overlooking its valley.

"Now he's gone," they replied, "the god of Haibori Mountain is no longer."

Could this terrestrial divinity (some of the villagers call it *dre* or ghost) be the original guardian divinity of this lovely valley? The old annals speak of Padmasambhava—the tantric yogi and magician who had compelled the earth divinities to act as protectors of the new Buddhist faith—as having come from Haibori to meet his patron, King Trisong Detsen, in advance of founding Samye *gompa*. They also tell of offering ceremonies -presumably there- to the *dra lha*, a pre-Buddhist warrior divinity often inhabiting just such a rocky place. In fact, the name of the prominent rocky mount is said to refer to the idea of panting, those panting breaths produced by its divinity on being chased by Padmasambhava.

Some, however, say that Haibori's divinity might be Pehar

himself, the pre-Buddhist deity who still manifests within the body of a monk at Nechung Monastery (now residing at the new Nechung *gompa*, in India). A shrine to Pehar had been erected early on at Samye *gompa*. After Samye's destruction, during the cultural revolution, Pehar's home continued to exist, but only on a subtle plane. Right now, however, monks at the old Nechung *gompa* near Lhasa are rebuilding his shrine for restoration at Samye.

After Padmasambhava determined the site of the monastery the workers' efforts were met with stiff spiritual resistance. The various spirit entities embodying the power and sentience of the land were not at all happy to have a Buddhist place built in the midst of their domain.

Initial pleas for their aid in building the monastery went unheeded. So Padmasambhava put his prodigious power to work and compelled them, through magical means, to carry rock and wood to the *gompa* site each night so that during the day the people could build it. It is said, he also required the *lü*, the serpent-tailed, *mer* gods and goddesses from the nearby Yarlung Tsangpo River, to give up some of their *norbu*, wealth and wish-granting jewels, to finance the undertaking.

Perhaps the god of Haibori still lives here, at this shuttered shrine building atop the pink granite summit of Haibori. Perhaps not. Still a hint of what his power must have been remains, if the rainbows of prayer flags and cairns of carefully placed stones—signs of prayers being made to the gods, Buddhist and aboriginal alike—are any indication.

Having survived a difficult magical birth, Samye *gompa* has endured down to the present time as a major crossroads of Tibetan spiritual life.

Samye *gompa* is both a physical and metaphysical structure, born out of a perspective focused upon the purified mind seeking enlightenment. *Samye* means, in fact, something like "Place of the Perfectly Contented Mind." It is conceived not only as a place of contemplation and ritual, but as a prime physical manifestation of the metaphysical.

It signifies, in its architectural plan, our entire universe according to the Buddhist conception of things. Samye *gompa* is, in fact, a great World *Mandala*, expressing the interconnected elements comprising the ideal version of our cosmos.

Its main building, the temple located at the center of the *gompa's* basically round precincts, is the material embodiment of holy Mount Meru, axis of our "world system." The round outer boundaries are likened to the impregnable iron mountain at the farthest limits of our universe.

The formerly existing, multileveled golden roofs— eradicated by the anger and ignorance of the cultural revolution and its roots—represented the various levels at which divine beings dwell atop the summit of Mount Meru. And, the entire building embodies their subtly seen, rainbow-colored palaces of clear light and glorious environments said to exist atop this most significant of the universe's "Pillars of the Sky."

Great doorways extend to the four directions from the temple-palace that is Samye. Beyond them once stood outer buildings and four great *chörten*, signifying the four world continents—each accompanied by two subsidiary ones—floating to the cardinal directions in a cosmic sea. We, it is said, inhabit the southern cluster of continents. Finally, among these outer structures are two smaller temples, dedicated to the sun and moon. In sum total they all provide the bare essentials of this "down to earth" Buddhist universe.

So, Samye Gompa stands not only at the crossroads of a beautiful valley and two faiths but, through the powers of the imagination, also at that of our entire universe.

It is a universe which explains, in symbolic terms, the structure of our external reality, using the imagery of the stable intersection of two crossed lines, enclosed by a circle. It also describes a plane midway between the infinity of the sky whose realm is pierced by the summit of the Cosmic Mountain and that of the depths of the earth.

In the process, the model upon which Samye *gompa* is patterned also provides a map of our internal reality.

It suggests the mental stability of two crossed lines (often conceived of as crossed *dorjes*, Diamond Scepters, which form the foundation of Mount Meru). It alludes to thoughts that branch out to all directions but which are protected and nurtured in the womb of the circle that is naturally described by them.

At their point of intersection sprouts the cosmic mountain of that limitless potential inherent within one's own consciousness. This suggests that one can achieve the compassion, clarity and omniscience of the buddhas, living atop lotus-shaped clouds at its summit, while having the physical form of one's being—like the mountain's base—firmly rooted in the process of living in the world.

The monks who chant and pray daily within Samye *gompa's* ancient halls know very well this inner meaning to their monastery. They know that they do not belong to simply any monastery, but are caretakers to the Axis of the Universe, at the Crossroads of Reality, atop the Altar of the Earth.

Their Old Tibetan Home

Donkadonka, donkadonka, bong! The animal bells send forth the unmistakable message that one is now far from the din and crush of Lhasa's city streets.

Instead, a certain quietness is all that one can hear. The village's adobe and stone dwellings, its inquisitive, smiling faces and slowly grazing livestock are a slow counterpoint to the city's frenetic scene.

They all provide a subdued yet exuberant welcome to Samye village, their Old Tibetan Home.

Just now a young villager and his cow—the source of the pleasant bell sounds—join an older woman and her young granddaughter in hovering over me as I sit on the edge of an irrigation ditch, at the margin between the villager's homes and their barley fields. Presently, they are joined by an old man, bent under a load of barley slung across his back, and two little girls, noses freely dripping. All have quietly surrounded me. They are intent upon this strange man's features and actions —especially his use of the left hand, out of which flies a riotous script only a bit more unintelligible to them than it is to him.

This is a place of unassuming stares; of a very real ease of being. Of living according to the natural rhythms of lightening and darkening; planting and harvesting; birthing and dying. Of fields of barley towered over by holy Haibori Hill. Of animals and people sending up a soft symphony matching, aurally, the subdued earth tones and soft shapes of their homes.

This is a village whose people are in tune with place and, in turn, with their inner selves and the greater cosmos beyond. It must have been here for a very long time. Certainly, some of the people's ancestors may have been living here at the time of Samye Monastery's founding in A.D.786, during the reign of King Trisong Detsen. The monastery was erected under the guidance of the great tantric master, Padmasambhava, to provide the monks the necessary solitude for their psychospiritual practices.

The people and their monastery live to the beat of an ancient drummer, one whose tattoo was almost stilled during the terror filled years of the cultural revolution, when the monastery was partially destroyed. Yet it seems as if it were meant to survive, despite the odds, given its significance as a place of learning and worship, and the obvious love, goodwill and probable protection by its village people.

If one takes the time and effort to see it, it becomes quite evident that monastery and village are not separate entities, but parts of a larger organism.

In Tibet, in fact anywhere in the world with its kind of religious tradition, the lay and monastic communities exist to the benefit of one another. One community retires from the exigencies of the physical world in order to enrich the other with its insights and spiritual activities; the other, in return for spiritual enrichment, provides the monks and lamas with help in their physical sustenance. They are—as in nature—in a dynamic symbiotic relationship with each other. And there is no better time than the present to see this partnership in action. These days, Samye *gompa* is alive with the sounds and motions of activity by both partners.

Inside the cool, dark halls the monks are intently chanting the compendium of sutra texts known as the *Kanjur*. Outside, atop the veranda, on the second storey, workers from the village clear the rubble accumulated over years of enforced neglect, since the "liberation." They make ready for the eventual replacement of its golden roofs, which had been destroyed in the zeal of the cultural revolution.

Inside the veranda, monk artisans make new statues to serve on the *gompa's* altars and they sew *appliqué* awnings to decorate and shade the monastery's many exposed alcoves.

Thus the villagers and monks work together to restore an historic, living entity that is both a symbol of a way of life and an active agent in an entire culture's mutually agreed upon goal of attaining enlightenment for themselves and all sentient beings.

Uh, oh, more company. Two teenaged girls and two older men have joined the crowd and their combined presence has shaken me from my reverie. Like the others, their eyes begin to follow, with fascination, the writing of these words.

I appreciate their friendliness and quiet inquisitiveness but it's not all that conducive to effective writing. Perhaps it's time to bid them all goodbye and begin my climb up Haibori Hill to see the shrine at its summit and get a bird's eye view of Samye *gompa*.

"*Dje yong, kale shu ah*" "sit slowly (goodbye), see you soon," I say, taking leave of them. I hope they can tell how much I've enjoyed their company and their Old Tibetan Home.

The Guru's Disciple

"The Great Guru has many names: Padmasambhava, Guru Rinpoche, Lopon Rinpoche, Urgyen Rinpoche, Nyima Ozer. Nyima Ozer actually grabbed the sun and ate all negativity that came his way." So explained the young Khampa pilgrim, Nyima, in the teahouse of the village surrounding Samye Monastery.

He gesticulated wildly, mimicking with uncanny accuracy the facial expressions and gestures which one sees time and again on statues and paintings of Tibetan divinities, particularly those with fierce demeanors and energies.

Nyima's name, meaning sun, is not the only point he shares in common with the Great Guru. If his actions and personality are any indication, he has become totally fixated upon that powerful tantric master who had sealed Buddhism in Tibet so long ago.

Guru Rinpoche is his *yidam*, his guiding and protecting tutelary deity. And in the course of his intense deity yoga, Nyima has, for all intents and purposes, become Padmasambhava.

In his intense identification with Guru Rinpoche, Nyima has begun to manifest that tantric willpower—in combination with a non-violent contrariness and unpredictability—necessary to engage obstacles and adverse conditions. The combination is a venerable tradition in Tibet, known as "crazy wisdom." Still, in a certain way, Nyima seems naive and vulnerable, as well.

Perhaps it's the result of having these qualities that Nyima seems to get along fine on next to no money, food or shelter as he continues his long pilgrimage to the holy places of Tibetan Buddhism.

I had first encountered Nyima on Lhasa's *barkhor*, its great circumambulation bazaar road and devotional path around the Jokhang, the holiest temple in Tibet. Nyima was a memorable sight, stripped to the waist as he executed grand prostrations on the worn flagstones that were covered with dust, animal excrement and various other sorts of undesirable refuse. But to Nyima it was all part of Padmasambhava's glorious Copper Colored Paradise of Urgyen.

Time and again arms extended over his head, hands together in a smooth, slow motion. His deep voice boomed out constant prayers and *mantras* as he spread out flat onto the street. On his back, over his shoulder, hung a *gahu*, a reliquary box. Through its glass window a painted image of the Great Guru peered out sternly. Also, depending from a strap over his shoulder hung three *phurba*. This magical dagger is particularly associated with the great magician who sealed Buddhism in Tibet by dispelling spiritual obstacles to its growth with its blade.

Even if I hadn't spoken with Nyima during the past few hours, I would certainly still have gotten the firm impression of his close, actually fanatical identification with the Great Guru.

How appropriate then to see Nyima at Samye Monastery. Whereas Samye is a necessary stop on any Tibetan Buddhist pilgrimage, for Nyima it holds an extra special meaning, considering that this first, classic Tibetan monastery was established in the latter part of the eight century under the guidance of Padmasambhava.

The person and event are remembered in the many statues and paintings of the Great Guru in the monastery's temple's halls and on its walls. One sees among them the usual Padmasambhava, with his firm and stern demeanor. But in the upstairs shrine room there is another Padmasambhava in residence. This statue shows a Guru Rinpoche whose mouth, teeth, lips and eyes convey that active, fierce quality which he manifested in the service of his spirituality on this very spot, twelve hundred years ago.

Nyima's actions and experience-worn face reveal a similar scenario: sometimes fierce, sometimes stern, sometimes kind but always intense. He has come to the place of his guru's holy work which—in the realm of mind, the universe that is the source of all matter and ideas—is as much his place as it is Padmasambhava's.

After all, ask Nyima if they aren't one and the same.

Trucking, "Tibetan Style"

The Khampa pilgrim, Nyima, who fully fancies himself at one with his divine *guru* Padmasambhava, has been chanting praises to his deity for about ten minutes now.

An old Tibetan man holds me tightly, his arm around my shoulders, while two women hang on to my jacket for dear life, much as I am doing to a random piece of metal and wood.

This is trucking, "Tibetan style."

The ramshackle lorry, owned by Samye Monastery, is making its bouncing half hour run to the ferry that will, in its own time, take us to the road connecting with Lhasa, three hours further down the line.

People crowd into the wooden flatboat, now empty but which, on an earlier run, was packed with sacks of barley, stacks of logs, nervous goats, sheep and even a calf. In short order, we are gliding across the sprawling Yarlung Tsangpo River. Despite the din of the gasoline engine, it is an placid and inwardly quieting journey. Within an hour we have arrived at the opposite muddy bank.

The ride has seemed like a vision. Arid mountains (perceptually small, but actually over sixteen thousand feet in height) stand out like glowing, tawny jewels against the gray-brown river and deep blue sky. One desires never to leave its smooth flow, especially considering the uncertainty of the next leg of the journey.

Will there be a truck awaiting us, or do we flag down a bus? Will we be stranded here and shall I miss returning in time to retain my room at the guest house in Lhasa?

Su hakogi re?. Who knows? Who cares!

Luckily, Kunchok, a young Tibetan from Sikkim, knows the answer, with certainty. His uncle's truck, driven by his cousin, will be meeting us. Sure enough, one can see the battered forest green lorry sitting silently in the distance, by the shore.

And soon begins the final leg of the pilgrimage by a truckload of Tibetans and a handful of Western travelers, between Tibet's oldest monastery and the sacred city of Lhasa, Place of the Gods.

I never cease to be amazed at how different it feels to be crowded together with Tibetans than with people of other nationalities. Indians, for example, dangle, and drape themselves saprophytically all over you, like spanish moss on the limbs of a tree. Tibetans, on the other hand, give you that extra bit of space, are actually considerate of each other's comfort despite being packed together, at times such as this, like sardines.

One wonders, in the midst of it all, what it would be like to be packed together with a crowd of Western business executives or suburban housewives, in a careening, open-backed truck. How would they relate to the crowding; the imprecise piles of sacks and bodies; the interminable dust and jolts of the earth and gravel road? No doubt, some might feel liberated from their involuntary bondage to illusory physical comforts. Most others, I fear, would be utterly horrified.

Just now, a party is in progress. We have stopped for petrol; trucks must eat and drink too, after all. And so must Tibetans; often at the most unusual times and places. The party's entertainment comes from a young Tibetan man who is putting on a show of drinking the alcoholic beverage, *chang*. Earlier, while the truck was still moving, he had succeeded in getting only a small portion of it into his mouth; the rest ran helter skelter down his shirt. Everyone had laughed. Now that we have stopped, he self-consciously slurps the brew with a disgustingly animated sound, to the delight of us all.

We are old and young; villagers and Lhasa-bred urbanites; and a few rough-edged Americans and complaining French tourists. As we bounce onward, we are rapidly congealing into one large family. It's always this way when people share difficult circumstances. And the thought arises that, in the West, instead of waiting for disasters or infrequent ritual occasions to bring us together, it might be done much more effectively by getting rid of airplanes, personal automobiles, and by de-paving the roads (or better yet, letting the "weeds" do it for us).

Think what fun it would be, bouncing along dusty roads, dressed in comfortable clothes, sharing each other's miseries and joys. Our interactive skills would drastically improve. We would no longer need dating services, singles bars or psychiatrists. We'd know how to naturally get close to one another, through the shared bases of experience and understanding.

I'm glad to be facing backwards in this careening truck. Besides making communication with the others easier, it prevents the dust and frequent pebbles from doing much damage to my exposed parts. It also prevents me from seeing any oncoming bus vying with the truck for space on this narrow road.

I sometimes write, sometimes converse, but mainly look around at the alternately arid, then cultivated countryside. The mighty Yarlung Tsangpo River, along whose flood plain the road winds, is the aorta of South Central Tibet. Its drainage system provides the life's blood of the land, the distillate of mineral rich mountains, food for the crops.

The intense sunlight at this high altitude and low latitude provides the rest of what is needed to grow the fattest, most luscious ears of barley to come out of human-assisted, natural selection.

Looking backward on the formidable scene, one realizes that despite its awesome austerity, it beckons maternally, like the Green Tara, Drolma Jangu, the supreme form of the Great

Goddess— Mother Nature—to whom every Tibetan Buddhist turns for solace and succor.

This is indeed her land. Infinitely bigger than human life yet nurturing of it. It's the breadbasket of Tibet, Heart of Asia.

Suddenly, the noisy, jostling rhythm stops. The ship of the road comes to an abrupt halt, fortunately under a grove of willow trees.

Blown tire. Such is reality in a land whose roads are rough and vehicle parts, scarce.

But what good fortune. To have a punctured inner tube along such a beautiful stretch of the Yarlung Tsangpo River is a blessing in disguise.

Some of our group prefer to await the repairs by lounging amid the bags and sacks atop the truck. Others (mainly the men) sit on the sand, under the trees, drinking *chang*, telling jokes and playing with scores of giant green caterpillars falling from the leaves.

Meanwhile the driver, aided by some passengers, makes magic with the inner tube. The original having been totally ruined, a spare with only two holes in it will have to do. Out comes the repair kit; pieces of the ruined inner tube will do as patches. Then comes an electric patch sealer, heated by the truck's battery. Then, almost magically, the tire is inflated with compressed air from somewhere within the truck's viscera. In the West, few truck drivers—not to mention private motorists— are capable of such improvisation. Tibetans would relate well to our sayings: "where there's a will, there's a way" and "necessity is the mother of invention."

While everyone's world revolves around the truck and tire, I take a walk. So much to see.

The sky is its usual intense lapis blue, suffused with plaques of cumulus clouds. They lie overhead, seemingly flat—like sheets of raw cotton— owing to the altitude of this highest major river system in the world.

The land is beige and sandy, with clumps of wildflowers and shrubs spaced at a distance from one another which makes walking among them most convenient. This is an arid land, despite its abundance of water. Looming above the valley floor—pinch me, am I awake?—rise a series of desert-like *mesas*. One need not even look askance to be transported to the high desert of the American Southwest. And rightly so, considering that the Navajo Indians who populate the American desert are clearly cousins of the Tibetans, sharing spiritual, lifestyle and linguistic attributes.

The tire work is now complete. The engine splutters and roars. Off we go. All is well. The truck is humming along. And now, as is often the case after periods of duress, everyone is enjoying each other's company all the more.

Especially Sharon from Boston. An old Tibetan woman has decided to mother her. Sharon has been having a difficult time getting comfortable in the anarchic pile of sacks and flesh. Now, as she lies across several people's legs, she has been given a sweater for a pillow and a wide-brimmed hat to cover her exposed arms and neck.

Ama-la, a chocolate-skinned and turquoise-studded grandmother, holds the hat carefully in place so that it doesn't jostle about. Sharon has just been adopted Tibetan style which basically means: "here, have some loving kindness; no big deal."

Imagine the scene. I sit against the leading wall of the truck's bed, with one foot lying lightly across Sharon's stomach. Luckily, it doesn't seem to bother her. Good thing, otherwise it would have no place to go. *Ama-la*, however, has other ideas for its placement. Suddenly, accompanied by a mischievious laugh, my heel is deftly placed, squarely within the depression of Sharon's crotch, to the uproarious delight of the entire truck!

A beaming *ama-la*, in the traditional Tibetan way of doing a greeting, sticks a pink tongue past her single ivory tooth. Thus haloed by her deeply lined, walnut-colored face she lets out several silent bellows at the impact of her wonderful prank.

Oh no, not again: the telltale hiss and flap of another flat tire! As we roll to a stop in a landscape equally as arid as the previous one, we notice a monastery sticking up from out of a stone and adobe village that looks more like the eroded hills than the work of human hands.

A monastery should not seem such an unusual sight here, but nowadays they are rare. The cultural revolution and the Chinese version of manifest destiny were the axes that almost severed Tibet's religious roots.

Taking advantage of this second stroke of good luck, we decide to continue our pilgrimage by visiting the monastery. And what luck it is. Gongkhar Chöde *gompa*, The Dharma Seat of Gongkhar Monastery, is slowly retaking its rightful place in the lives of the people of the village and district of Gongkhar. Seriously damaged and looted a generation ago, it is slowly being restored, painfully so, as money is quite scarce. Fortunately, the people are willing to help and like many monasteries in today's Tibet, it echoes with the reassuring sounds of work.

This is a gem of a monastery, even in its state of ill repair. Superb frescoes of tantric deities and fierce protectors grace its walls. A colorful, silk brocade-filled chanting hall serves villagers from the entire area. It is now an ecumenical *gompa*. Originally established as a Sakya monastery it, like many of today's monasteries, serves several of Tibet's buddhist sects, now that so many *gompas* have been destroyed.

The work activity here testifies to the effect of currently liberalized policies toward religious worship by the Chinese. Whether it will remain so, is hard to tell. But one realizes, too, that given the indomitable spirit and clear-headedness of the Tibetans, the spirit of Tibet will likely prevail.

"Great Drolma, Savioress of all Beings, Mother of the Buddhas, we beseech you for your aid."

I'm quite sure that prayers such as this are currently running through the minds of the people on this rickety pilgrim truck. With its now unfixable flat tire (fortunately there's a paired wheel next to it) and an engine that sounds like a meatgrinder at work on a handful of iron nails, we pull up, limpingly, to Drolma *lhakhang*, God's House of the Drolmas." Only seventeen kilometers from Lhasa!

A more auspicious arrival could not have been planned.

What should have been a three hour trip has taken eight, during which time we were certain that the truck would never make it. Somehow, inexplicably, it managed to grind onward. Perhaps it was the pilgrims' prayers to Drolma that saved the day.

So here we stand, not a little unsteadily, poised to enter Tibet's most important shrine to the Great Goddess. Within, sit twenty-one statues of Drolma, each possessing the energy of one of her twenty-one emanations and qualities of consciousness. They are said to bestow their blessings upon all who make the pilgrimage here. Likewise the entire God's House is sacred, having been built by the great eleventh century teacher, Atisha as a place from which to give his teachings.

This has been a most auspicious journey.

It's a happy time of day to be out and about. It's seven thirty in the evening and the sun is still strong and high in the sky as the truck clunks its way up the Kyichu (Waters of Happiness) Valley. And though I've been along this route before, a certain thrill begins to arise at the prospect of returning to Lhasa.

Who said a pilgrimage would be easy? Not easy but, when done in the Tibetan style, a most pleasurable experience.

LHASA
PLACE OF THE GODS

"You run so fast and can't be seen
like the sound of hidden temple horns;
my beautiful horse, Pintsok.
I fondly recall those better days
prayer flags fluttering white, atop the Potala
my beautiful horse, Pintsok.
Fire is born from earth
and the land of fire is aflame;
oh, my beautiful Pintsok."
　　　　—from a contemporary Tibetan folksong

The Jokhang

Tour de Force in the House of the Lord

They had tried it before, to build a sacred space on Wothang Tso—the Lake upon the Milky Plain—but to no avail. Only after Queen Bhikruti Devi had gathered the necessary skilled workers and materials, and had arranged for the spirits of the lake not to interfere, was it assured of success.

Her husband, the great *Dharma* King Songtsen Gampo, had determined the lake to be an auspicious site for the temple by throwing his ring into its waters. It is said that where the ring landed there materialized a white *chörten*, and that the lake still exists below the courtyard of the resulting *tsuklak-hang*, the House of Mysteries*. Inside this grand cathedral, like a jewel in a golden setting, sits the Jokhang, House of the Lord, and its sacred statue of Sakyamuni Buddha, focal point of all Tibetans' prayers and personal pilgrimages.

They come daily, by the thousands, crowding the tiny chapels and their shrines to saints and buddhas, here in the sacred city.

With butterlamps and prayer wheels, *khatag* greeting scarves and prayer beads in their hands and *mantras* on their lips, the pilgrims enter each successive shrine room in the innermost sanctum of this cathedral of the enlightened mind.

They add clarified butter to the great glowing butterlamps

that, until the recent advent of the electric light, were the only source of light (in the material sense, that is) in this dramatic, cave-like space, whose paintings, statues, relics and architectural details blend into an ambience of mystery.

My pilgrimage to the House of the Lord, within the House of Mysteries, at the Place of the Gods, atop the Altar of the Earth is about to begin. I will embark upon a clockwise cycle walked by countless others during the twelve centuries that the House of Mysteries has been in existence.

Its great sandalwood and metal doors have been opened to admit this morning's deluge of pilgrims. They stream past a huge metal prayer wheel, many times the height of the old and young pilgrims walking alongside it and turning it. They burst into the courtyard assembly area and through another set of great doors, into the Jokhang proper. They find themselves in the Jokhang's inner chanting hall and begin their clockwise pilgrimage within. I follow.

My first stop is the shrine room containing the statues of Tsong Khapa, the great fifteenth-century founder of the yellow-hatted Gelug sect of Tibetan Buddhism, and his eight disciples among whom were the founders of some of Tibet's major monasteries. Although this temple is an ecumenical one—possessing things sacred to all the sects—it is a main provenance of the Dalai Lamas, who are the *de facto* heads of the Gelug order. Understandably, Tsong Khapa holds a prominent position in this population of saints and buddhas.

"*Om Mani Padme Hung, Om Mani Padme Hung*" bubbles from their lips as the pilgrims touch the crowns of their heads to the wooden receptacles in which sit the saints and teachers' statues. This physical act is matched by their inner vision as they link up with the divine awareness imbued within the statues, and which is simultaneously arising within their own minds.

Onward the pilgrims surge. I follow, somewhat bewildered by this, my first tour through the Jokhang.

A young Tibetan monk approaches me and volunteers that the next chapel contains the statues and healing powers of the

Men Lha, the Eight Medicine Buddhas. Each is, I recall, an emanation of the original Medicine Buddha, healer of all afflictions, be they physical, karmic, psychological or the results of spirits' malevolence. But never has my experience of the Medicine Buddha been so intense, even in my weak imagination, as at this moment when I am packed into this tiny shrine room with over a dozen shuffling pilgrims. One can feel the Medicine Buddha's healing power as it impregnates the chapel and courses through the pilgrims' bodies and minds. It all has the effect of integrating one's entire being. Of becoming whole. "Holy."

If the previous chapels seemed crowded then now must come the crunch. The line begins to form in earnest as we come upon the next shrine room dedicated to Thukje Chenpo, Chenrezi (the bodhisattva Avalokiteshvara) in his eleven-headed, thousand-armed form. This is a very holy statue which through sanctification, prayer and the baptism of visualized thoughts, embodies the active principle of the Buddha's compassion. It is also a significant symbol to Tibetans since each Gwalya Rinpoche, otherwise known by his Mongolian title of Dalai Lama, is the incarnation—the emanation in a perceivable form—of this quality of the buddha mind.

Understandably, in Tibet, where spiritual devotion and energy are particularly strong, lines are equally long.

The throngs of pilgrims ebb but mainly flow as we come to the chapel of Chamba Trutse, Maitreya, the Coming Buddha.

It is said that every major age has its enlightened human teacher who manifests during the darkest days of degeneration. Indeed, there have been many previous buddhas over the eons but only three are "on record" during this *kalpa* or world eon. The most recent one was called Sakyamuni, Sage of the World. All indications are that another degenerate age is cycling around. And residing ready, in his paradisic buddha field, is Chamba- Maitreya. He's envisioned as a splendidly outfitted buddha—as are all enlightened beings said to appear in their subtle realms—realms composed out of the rainbow-colored, clear light of mental energy. He sits upon a throne in the Western fashion, as if in a chair. Some lamas say that this may signify that Chamba will emanate and teach the *dharma* in the West. Let's hope so.

Lhasa urbanites, nomads, village farmers, monks and nuns all press together now gracefully and calmly. They create an overwhelming sensory brew of mumbling and cantillating sounds; fermented body and yak butter aromas; and woolen and silk, turquoise and coral bedecked forms in quest of an enlightened mind.

Many, in the thickly growing line, carry lit butterlamps as the illuminated procession files past another statue of Je Rinpoche(Tsong Khapa), then through a chapel dedicated to the sacred lake beneath its floors, and into a shrine of Öpame, (known in Sanskrit as Amitabha), the Buddha of Boundless Light.

The great butterlamps within the latter send out a warm orange glow, illuminating the statue of the orange-red bodied tantric buddha from whose mental continuum so many other tutelary divinities emanate. He is the Buddha of Boundless Light because he dwells in a glowing, orange-red paradise, situated in the western cardinal direction, realm of the setting sun. The name is also particularly appropriate because he embodies the essence of meditative insight, that which creates a warm inner glow as one increasingly recognizes the nature of the enlightened mind.

But all the spiritual light that one has so far experienced is about to pale. The energy in and around the glorious statue of the Jo Rinpoche begins to exude a tremendous glow to the eyes of both the body and mind.

Here, at the focal point of the pilgrimage to the ultimate God's House, sits the Jo statue, formed in the tantric image of Sakyamuni. With a crown and vestment of gold and precious jewels, signifying his existence in the *sambhogakaya* realm, the "adorned, enjoying body" state of being, this visage of Sakyamuni can only be seen, it is said, by divine beings and highly evolved humans with the clarity of inner sight developed over long years on the path toward enlightenment.

The Jo Rinpoche is much more than a consummate art work or holy relic. It is the enlightened mind made manifest. It signifies that which we too may attain through concentrated effort along the "Diamond Path" of *Vajrayana* Buddhism.

Here, perhaps more than anywhere that I have so far been upon the Altar of the Earth, does the totally consuming nature of the religion shine forth. Here is evidence of an entire nation working toward enlightenment so as to help all other beings gain the necessary awareness to join them there.

The flickering light, throbbing prayers and presence of the great statue bring me into a special state of mind, causing me to write these words in a stream of consciousness way.

In the mysterious darkness there is light.

Things on the Altar of the Earth are larger than life. Not only the mountains and sky, but the statues, sacred objects and people's energy in God's Houses such as this are of a magnitude beyond normal proportions.

The air feels electric on entering the shrine of the Jo Rinpoche. The pilgrims' demeanors are reverently intense as they leave money and, temporarily, their butterlamps upon the altar before the sacred statue. The Jo glows with that light which can only come from flame being reflected off gold and jewels. All shuffle clockwise around it. The massive statue of a fierce divinity guards the walkway; he jumps out at the perception of the pilgrim. Arm and hand extended, he protects the Jo statue and all who enter its refined realm. He is one of two in this *lhakhang*, "God's House" of the Jo. They are: Tamdrin, the "horse-necked" *dharma* protector and Chana Dorje, a manifestation of the skilled power component of the Buddha's mind.

Other huge, gilded forms stand sentry over the moving throngs. They are the buddhas and bodhisattvas who populate the Jo Rinpoche's pure realm. In the course of this holiest of circumambulations one cannot help but sense the message that it so patently imprints on the mind. That here among glowing buddhas in their physical—though least refined—forms, is a hint of what may come to one's mind if it is allowed to realize its own buddha light.

Then, as suddenly, we are out of the inner sanctum. The pilgrims retrieve their burning butterlamps and our little group steps back into the darkness.

Walking, or is it floating, we pass another chapel of Maitreya. Such a beautiful face. Let's hope it augers well for the coming enlightened age. Then, past another shrine to Chenrezi and we suddenly arrive at a stairwell that articulates with the mezzanine. Up the stairs, at the end of a long, dark corridor, we come to a place of energy that is equally dark yet dedicated to light.

In the dim butterlamp light a monk sits before a huge, doubleheaded drum, incessantly intoning prayers. He is watched over by incredibly crafted statues of fierce looking tantric tutelary deities and protectors of the religion. I can—I think—recognize two. One is Naljorma or Vajra Yogini. She is the psychic temptress who attracts one's lustful impulses then utilizes them to "slay" one's ego.

The other appears to be of a class of archaic protectors of the religion known as *chökyong*, or *dharmapala*, in Sanskrit. This one looks very much like the fierce divinity Pehar who had advised the Dalai Lamas on affairs of the state through the medium of a monk-oracle at Nechung Monastery, a few kilometers up the Lhasa Valley.

Protector's House chapels are always dark and dramatic places, having a distinctly mysterious air about them. And this *gönkhang* seems to be a powerful beacon to the pilgrims who can be heard intoning the protector divinities' names and various *mantras* as they exit the chapel.

Some chapels are closed. Perhaps it's not appropriate to view their indwelling divinities; perhaps it's an inappropriate time of year, or they are restricted from the view of uninitiated eyes. Other chapels, one suspects, no longer contain their holy relics. There are many mysteries in the House of Mysteries.

The young monk who "adopted" me at the beginning of my rounds proposed a mutually beneficial arrangement. I was to write down the name of each chapel and deity in English transliteration and liberally sprinkle it with the more recognizable Sanskrit names. In this way he could inform tourists of the contents of the Jokhang without having to know English. In turn, he would be my guide, answer my questions and would patiently wait for me to scribble out the antecedents to this essay.

One good turn deserves another; karma in action.

Despite not stopping at each and every chapel I am quite satisfied with the tour that I, and now you, have been taking. To miss a few shrine rooms but to capture the flavor of the Jokhang's sublimity is quite an acceptable trade off. Anyway, the other chapels await you and I, at a later date.

But there is much more yet to come. In another hidden corner of the mezzanine one finds oneself among beings of great mental power.

First, it's on to the chapel of Padmasambhava, who enlisted the aid of indigenous deities, such as one might see in the previous chapel, as protectors of the new faith.

Equally fierce in demeanor as the protector deities but working toward a most gentle end, are some of the tantric tutelaries. One of the most important is Demchok, known as Samvara in Sanskrit. His chapel sits to the right of Padmasambhava's. He is the emblem of one of the most important lineages of mental and physical practices in the *Vajrayana*, the tantric buddhist path of rapid mental development. But Demchok is also a divinity of the land, living as he does in a *mandala*, a palatial temple of clear light, atop Mount Kailas, holiest mountain in Tibet since pre-buddhist times.

Demchok, whose statue glows behind a glassed-in alcove, is represented in the *yab-yum* (father-mother) attitude of the male divinity "sporting" in union with his complementary female reflex, Prajnaparamita, The Goddess of the Perfection of Wisdom. Demchok thus radiates to all who comes his/her way with those ideal qualities attainable along the Diamond Path to enlightenment.

Things are beginning to once again intensify as the line of pilgrims congests a narrow flight of stairs, in order to behold two revered statues of their greatest protector goddess, Palden Lhamo. These are quite unlike the forms in which she is usually depicted. Normally, she is shown as a very fierce, blue skinned and fanged being, wielding skulls, and weapons; blood, skin and fire everywhere. She is the powerful female energy that protects Lhasa, the Tibetan state and, particularly, the Dalai Lamas.

Here, in the hub of the Place of the Gods, she is shown in two rarer guises. The lefthand statue is utterly inhuman and indescribably fierce in demeanor, with huge bulging eyes and a gaping grin. In her other form she is much more placid by comparison, though hardly calming. She wears a jeweled tantric headdress, signifying the adorned," enjoying body" state of buddhahood. Her abundant silvered teeth reveal her fierce compassion for the Tibetan people. Given the current state of affairs in Tibet, I suspect I know what kind of prayers these pilgrims are uttering before her.

Breaking the spell, the young monk quickly spirits me down the stairs to the ground floor and another Padmasambhava shrine. Then it's on to another Chamba chapel. In its corner is a small, sculpted form of the "mystic sacred goat," which is directly linked with the legend of the building of the Jokhang. It tells of an indefatigable female goat who carried the earth and stone used to build the great structure.

Next in line is a shrine to the healing powers of the Eight Medicine Buddhas and another to Öpame-Amitabha, Buddha of Boundless Light.

Continuing clockwise around the walkway we come to a chapel dedicated to the "Seven Buddha Successors" and one to nine statues of Tsepame, Buddha of Boundless Life, an active, bodhisattva form of Öpame. After this one, comes a chapel dedicated to the three deities who jointly embody the energy needed to insure a long life. They are Tsepame, with his energy of long life; Namgyelma, Goddess of Long Life; and Drolma or Tara, the wish-fulfilling Mother of the Buddhas.

Finally, we arrive at the chapel of the great king Songtsen Gampo and of Thomni Sambhota, his scholar-emissary to India who formulated the Tibetan alphabet in the seventh century, facilitating the preservation of Buddhism in Tibet.

Outside this shrine, a wall mural depicts the mystic goat, the gold ring thrown by Songtsen Gampo into the lake below the Jokhang and the magical, white *chörten* which arose on the spot where it landed.

Suddenly, comes the sensation of light, as we find ourselves back in the chanting hall among the great statues of Chenrezi, Padmasambhava and Chamba. But before going up to the roof, the young monk wants to make certain that I do not miss anything on this level and we visit two more alcoves that are on either side of the vestibule leading into the Jokhang proper. They hold an imposing array of statues of the most archaic class of earth divinities of Tibet, those who had been brought into the Buddhist fold, early on, as protectors. They include the the female serpent-shaped spirits of the watery places, the *lümo*, and the sometimes fierce protectors of mountainous places, the *neuchen*. They serve here to protect this most holy of Tibet's shrines.

Having covered the lower levels of the Jokhang to his satisfaction my monastic guide leads me up to the roof, retracing earlier steps past the Palden Lhamo statues and into the *pelchok dukhang*, a chanting hall dedicated to the protectors and tantric tutelary deities. Its walls and altars are encrusted with paintings and other images of these divine embodiments of the forces of the mind.

Huge drums hang in place over long, narrow carpeted benches, made ready for a coming ceremony. Here the most powerful divinities and their concomittant states of mind are invoked on behalf of the monks' as well as all beings' enlightenment.

The ambience is one of a great cool presence.

At the same time, another environmental quality makes itself felt. Just over there, the bright Tibetan sunlight slashes through a doorway leading to the roof. I know from earlier photographs that this will be an utterly different experience from that within, but one equally as infinite. It is a place with a panoramic view resulting in the kind of inspiration that aided in creating all that I have seen within the House of the Jo.

The sky is very clear, with but a few cumulus clouds crowning the sixteen thousand foot high peaks dominating the city and valley. There, glinting in the distance, on Red Mountain Hill, floats the Potala, the temple-palace of Chenrezi who, in his physical form, is the Dalai Lama. It looks like a kind of gold and glacier-topped mountain jutting up out of an ocean of old earth-toned Tibetan buildings that are festooned in rainbows of prayer flags and colorful awnings. And without much mental effort, one is carried to its heights from this perch atop the Jokhang.

And arising too, just now, is a feeling of great thankfulness that there was room enough for one more pilgrim, here in the House of the Lord.

* My special thanks to Keith Dowman for his translation of the word *tsuklakhang*.

The Sounding of Tibet

How different the sounds, but how equally primal. And how basic to a total way of life.

From the second storey of the Jokhang, one can hear it all in a sacred and secular symphony combined.

Just now, in the courtyard below, the tinkles of the hand-held *drilbu* bells fire the empty space like successive waves of the sea washing against lonely beaches. Or, are they wind chimes set into frenzied motion by the same hurricane's gale?

A few minutes ago the echoing sounds, given life by the monks, were less meditative, more powerful. They were calling up an appropriate mental state associated with the particular tantric divinity being invoked in the day-long *shapten*, a ceremony on behalf of the family sitting patiently in attendance.

The crow's cry of the reedy shawms, the tintinabulating cymbals, the drums' earthy throbs, are precise, profound, intense and, to some, even brash. But their few tones and subtle rhythms succeed in carrying one into a universe of divine beings. One is borne on sonorous wings to their temples, floating on lotus-shaped clouds atop an awesome cosmic mountain. It's a place even well above Lhasa, the Place of the Gods.

But there are other sounds that simultaneously carry the at-

tention to differing heights. Unlike the monastic sounds that
bear one to rainbow-lit temples of divinities (and, equally, their
places within our minds), these sounds point to a spot scarce-
ly a few meters above me.

Several Tibetan women are dancing and singing while they
work. They are making a new roof for the Jokhang's third
and topmost storey. Like all Tibetan-style earthen roofs this
one needs to be tamped down in order to resist the effects of
the weather.

With stout tamping rods (wooden sticks with circular discs
of stone affixed at the bottom ends), they tamp the roof down.
And as they tamp they stamp their feet. They dance a dance
in work-time, to the accompaniment and exhortation of lovely tunes. Their open, reedy voices are *au naturel*: not the
studied, high pitched litanies of Tibetan opera singers or the
mesmeric, earth-shaking growls of the monks. Simply natural sounds from natural people, doing what comes naturally.

By chancing to sit between these sounds I have come to appreciate the full range of what it is to be Tibetan. It goes from
an earthy, open-hearted, "whistle while you work" approach
to living to deeply introspective and serious soundings in the
service of the spirit. It's a way of satisfying the needs of the
world without, while inspiring the spirit within.

Resounding

The monks of the Jokhang are offering resounding prayers tonight, amid glorious buddha fields.

Their mesmeric chants blend organically with massive statues dominating the chanting hall. The chants bounce echoingly against ancient, elaborately carved columns and lintels; through groves of precise *thangka* paintings depicting deities and Sakyamuni Buddha's life, and around great silk brocade banners emblazoned with celestial dragons.

They breeze too, about the 108 braids of Amdo nomad women's hair, the turquoise and coral bedecked necks of Khampa villagers, and the silk-clothed bodies of Lhasaites, all here to receive the blessings of the evening *shapten*, ceremony.

The repetitive sounds set the busy mind into a smoother groove, clearing out extraneous thoughts while invoking the presence of buddhas, bodhisattvas and enlightened teachers who simultaneously exist in their paradises atop the cosmic mountain at the center of our universe—Mount Meru—and here, in Tibet's holiest sacred space.

At the same moment, the resounding litany of the *Lama Chöba* ceremony brings to mind more earthly realities, out of two ignoble times in the history of Tibet. One was that difficult period of religious persecution during the reign of the notorious early king, Langdarma, who had temporarily banished Buddhism from the land.

This ceremony is a vivid metaphor to this era's revival of the religion, after similar persecution by a more powerful potentate. For with each successive strophe of the chant, Buddhism reasserts itself ever more strongly in the psyche and actions of the Tibetan people.

"May the center reassert itself," their chants seem to say, "with the stability of the cosmic peak at the universe's center. And may the *dharma* rain fall equally, to the four directions on the Altar of the Earth and throughout this vast universe, for the betterment of all beings."

Deeply planted seeds
burst forth freshly
on fire-scarred forest land.

Monasteries

Phoenix from the Ashes

"There's an old saying among Tibetans," Yeshe began, as we crawled unsteadily from the open-backed truck after a torturous ride up the mountainside to Ganden Monastery.

"When a person has difficulties at the beginning of a pilgrimage, we say it brings the kind of good fortune that wipes away previous sins and misfortunes."

Yeshe's attitude is one which Tibetans carry with them throughout life, moderating its hardships and keeping them mindful of its joys. It's a certain resolute optimism and a willingness to encounter, endure and transcend the sometimes stark reality of living. Life's inevitable problems and pitfalls are things they understand all too well in their experiences on the rugged Plateau of Tibet and through the teachings of Buddhism.

Ironically, it was both the land and their religion which drew the wrath of the Chinese (we often hate and fear that to which we are attracted, but cannot understand). Still, every Tibetan knows that in the long run the land and religion will be their salvation.

No greater symbol can be found, of both the devastation and the Tibetans' will to survive, than in the current revival of Ganden *gompa*, The Solitary Place of Joy.

Ganden is like the mythic phoenix bird—a prideful symbol of people in this part of the world—whose plumage flashes in the sunlight of a new day dawning, as it rises unscathed from the ashes of a fiery holocaust.

Ganden Monastery's story is all too common knowledge. The majority of its carefully built stone structures had all been in ruin six or seven years ago when, Yeshe relates, "it was like a ghost village. Some people say that you were able to hear the sad spirits crying out in anguish during the night."

The dynamite and cannons of the People's Liberation Army, while liberating one piece of stone masonry from another, failed to destroy the mortar of mind and spirit which bound them together.

So Ganden was destined to re-arise, phoenix-like from its own ashes through voluntary labor and donations by lay and monastic Tibetans and now, it is said, reparations from the Chinese.

Understandably, Ganden is a potent symbol of the revival of the entire Tibetan identity. Practically every pilgrim to Central Tibet packs into an incredibly uncomfortable bus or truck for the essential journey to this sacred place and its special state of mind.

Today it's my turn. I've joined Yeshe, his family and friends for a pilgrimage to the Place of Joy.

Come along with us!

Our pilgrimage begins at the psychospiritual heart of the phoenix. The Sertong *lhakhang*, the Golden Tomb God's House, is a fortress-like, red stone building that dominates this mountainside of ruins and rebuilt structures.

It takes its name from the golden *chörten* within, which holds the remains and mental essence of Tsong Khapa, the monastery's founder and spiritual master of the Gelug order of Tibetan Buddhism. This is the most hallowed space at Ganden; no wonder, then, the Sertong *lhakhang's* fortress-styled architecture.

One enters the shrine room by way of a chanting hall which,

today, is alive with the ceremonial chants of several hundred monks. They have returned to Ganden on their own volition, to rebuild and administer the sacred space and its contents.

As in old Tibet, the Sertong *lhakhang* has become a bee-hive of activity. In a courtyard on the ground level, artisan monks and laymen are busy at work forming clay statues of fierce protectors of the Buddhist religion. Such protective ener-gy is definitely called for, considering the tragic history of the Place of Joy. Beyond the courtyard, in a chapel, comes the beat of a great ceremonial drum, deep chants of the monks, glints of darkly flickering butterlamps and the deep musky aroma of it all.

Presently, a steep stairway conducts us to the second floor and an entirely different sort of religious activity. There, an old monk makes *tsampa* (roasted barley flour) impressions of a human tooth, set into an old, silver, *chörten*-shaped base. It is said to be one of Tsong Khapa's own molars! Tiny tabs of grain dough, bearing the molar's impression, spit out of the monk's dexterous hands. They are "long life" edible com-munion for Ganden's pilgrims, their families and friends. Aided by sufficiently strong belief, they are said to work wonders for one's health and welfare.

Quitting the Golden Tomb God's House, our party wends its way through the rubble to an adjacent red-washed, stone building. It houses a library of *pecha*, the essential religious texts, containing teachings by the Buddha and other deities, as well as commentaries on them by revered ancient teachers. The texts have a sacrosanct aura about them. They are consi-dered to be the Buddha's speech faculty, much as the statues and *thangka* paintings inside the Sertong *lhakhang* are synony-mous with his body; and the *chörten*, his mind.

The next building along the path is revered for the body, speech and mind of a more temporal teacher. It contains the seat of the abbot of Ganden, the Tri Rinpoche (successor to Tsong Khapa), in the form of a throne and special ritual ob-jects. Like all else here, the throne was destroyed during the cultural revolution and has been newly made to ancient specifications.

The present Ganden Tri-pa now resides in India, at his seat in the newly established Ganden Monastery, located in a refugee community in the south of the country.

Two Gandens? Yes. Why not? Things are not linear and mutually exclusive in the realm of absolute, formless reality, after all. One is but a natural extension of the other, as are a temple and its statues (indeed, all phenomena) ultimately material constructs of conceptions existing within the mind. Ganden will coexist in a cloned state until the parts can be rejoined in harmony and peace.

Yeshe seems pensive as we exit an upstairs shrine room dominated by a statue of Demchok, the great tantric guardian who holds forth from the summit of Mount Kailas, Tibet's holiest peak. Yeshe quietly exclaims that, in the twenty-seven years since he's left Ganden—as a thirteen-year-old monk (in 1959, before its destruction)—the changes have been so monumental as to be "beyond belief."

Never having been here, but having seen the old photographs of Ganden before its destruction, I was likewise left speechless. One can only speculate on its full impact upon Yeshe, a longtime refugee on his first visit home.

Some of the buildings, those so far restored from out of their broken walls and foundations' rubble, house the monks now in residence. And one building, appropriately situated at the top of the once bustling monastic city, has special meaning for all pilgrims, especially Yeshe.

This is the Lübum *khang*, the House of One Hundred Thousand Nagas. *Nagas* or *lü* are powerful spirit dwellers of the watery realms who hold the key to happiness and wealth in the form of *norbu*, wish-fulfilling jewels. The Lübum is Tsong Khapa's original dwelling, recently rebuilt. And just beside it, still in ruins, is Yeshe's former home.

Like Tsong Khapa, Yeshe's father had been born in the northeastern Tibetan province of Amdo and, as is the custom, the monks of Yeshe's *dratsang*—monastic house—all had an Amdo connection. "Birds of a feather," as it were. Not surprisingly, the Lübum *khang* was recently restored by the people of Amdo.

The vertical climb, at an altitude of fourteen thousand feet, now essentially completed, we and seven pilgrims just in from Amdo are treated to buttered tea in the Lübum's kitchen, served up by an Amdo-born monk. The tea is definitely in order, particularly since the next strenuous facet of the pilgrimage is about to begin.

Like many of Tibet's sacred places, Ganden sits atop a mountain. And where there's a sacred mountain and atop it, a sacred shrine, one can be certain that there's a footpath winding around it. This is the *lingkhor*, the circumambulation trail on which one leaves offerings and partakes of the spiritual energies of the place.

Entering onto the *lingkhor* brings one into a spiritual communion of a different complexion than that experienced within the monastery. Here there is a powerful connection with the sentience of the earth—a more ancient strain of spirituality than the formalized expressions of spirit, glowing within the monastery's walls.

The trail skirts the mountainside as hardly more than a scratch on its rocky skin. Across a saddle ridge looms the sacred mountain Angönri, a great green and brown giant.

The trail winds past incised boulders bearing *mantras* that invoke Buddhist divinities whose qualities already potentially exist within the pilgrims' own minds.

On rounding the first big bend, it is as if one has just walked onto a grand stage whose backdrop is more real than reality. The great, broad, mountain-studded Kyichu River valley snaps fully into view in all its magnificence.

Browns, grays, beiges, blues and whites: mountains, touching clouds, make bends in riverine flows; valleys stretch lazily into infinity.

And rocks. And flowers. And patches of *ganden khempo*—tiny aromatic herbs growing low to the ground—a prized form of incense throughout Tibet.

And more rocks. Boulders, escarpments and extrusions.

Rocks, rocks and more rocks.

Rocky shrines dot the trail. Within them, the rock faces have taken on faces and figures all their own. They are *rangchung* visions, "self-arising" images of deities and protectors. Some are more clearly formed than others in the raw, native rock-face; helped along, no doubt, by the touch of countless fingers, stroking them over the centuries with sincere devotion.

Here's a protector of the religion. There. . .well, I'm not quite sure whom it is. It's too early to tell. Perhaps in another fifteen or twenty years it will have manifested more clearly.

The trail has been quite level up to this point. But suddenly, Yeshe's sister Drolkhar (the "White Tara") takes us on an uphill detour toward a long slab of slick, black rock.

"This is the Vision Rock," Drolkhar explains. "You clench your fist and look at the rock through the tiny aperture formed between your palm and fingers. Then you will see a vision."

Yeshe sees a village, fields and mountain slopes in the rock's hide. I, alas, see a rock. A "Place of Joy," populated by budd-has in palaces of rainbow-colored light, floating atop lotus shaped-clouds, would have been preferable.

Taking the trail downslope, we soon approach a small hillock seeming to jut out into the void spreading beyond the distant valley.

"Shall we go to the sky burial site?" comes the basically rhetorical question. My answer, as that of the others, is a resounding,"of course!" I am motivated by intense curiosity for this singularly unusual way of disposing of the dead, but I also want a way of experiencing something of the ambience of this joining of the body with the infinite sky realm without having to impinge upon the privacy of an ongoing event—a growing problem in Tibet, given the curious tourists.

How very strange, these greasy rocks and the watery pool surrounding them, stained red, clearly with blood. And the strong lymphatic odor, as well as the nearby pile of ash, liberally salted with scattered human bones. The cremation mound testifies, I am told, to the current inauspicious inability of the vultures to complete their age-old work.

And the knives; a dozen or more in various stages of rusting. And that single shiny one. All have been left on location after the flaying job was done. The shiny one belongs, it seems, to that recent event which left the telltale pool of red liquid.

As the bizarreness of the place slowly wears off, I am reminded that it is, in fact, a potentially excellent place, given the Tibetans' healthy views on death and dying.

The sky burial is a necessary stop along this pilgrimage route since it reminds one, in its vivid way, of the mental necritude that must be cast off in the course of one's lifetime. In fact, I've been told that people often roll about or actually do somersaults here in order to scrape themselves clean of any "sins" or mental defilements. The idea is that such impediments to enlightenment and earthly happiness would be left for disposal at the charnel ground, along with the grosser, physical forms.

The defilements now theoretically disposed of, there comes the time to find the spot where the success of the work may be tested.

Once again we go uphill from the main trail and arrive at what can perhaps be best described as the Gauge of Sins. It consists of two large boulders which look almost as if they were once one, but were rudely split in two, then separated, by some monstrous hand. The "crack" is just wide enough for an average person to negotiate. Its form is uneven and, in many places, very slippery due to years of wear. So passage along its gauntlet is not a purely straightforward affair. And that's just how its purpose as a sin gauge is served.

To Tibetans, omens and signs—tied as they are to mental qualities and karma—are everything. The state of one's system and one's immediate actions and their results are clearly linked. So, the ease or difficulty with which one passes through the Gauge of Sins' rocks, suggests the current effects upon the state of one's body and mind by previous thoughts and deeds.

Fortunately, we all pass through it uneventfully. Perhaps we had shed sufficient obstacles during our visit to the sky burial site.

Thus purified and diagnosed, we continue onto our next major stop. We pilgrims are now a tightly knit group. Together, we've snaked our way along the dark, yak butter-saturated passageways of the phoenix-arisen buildings. Then along a sometimes perilous rocky trail skirting their mountainside, as if a single organism with many freely moving limbs.

We now come to one of the concluding episodes of our pilgrimage and silently enter the cave where Tsong Khapa (who had founded Ganden *gompa* in 1409) had habitually meditated.

"Here," the attending monk explains, "certain miracles were performed by Je Rinpoche (his honorific title)." These included pulling a huge boulder up out of "free-fall." In so doing, the marks from his grasping fingers were left clearly visible in the rock face.

The cave's rocky walls are alive, as well, with self-arisen deity figures. They are highlighted with bright colors in the inimitable Tibetan fashion, making them seem, in the right light, like rainbow arrays of wallflowers.

The cave has become, like so many hermitages of great Tibetan saints, a major pilgrimage place. Certainly the combined awe of the visitors and stories by the attending monk reinforce the sacred ambience of this shrine.

Now that we are well around the mountain trail's final bend, the monastery is again within view. One more stop for one more ritual experience is in order here.

This shiny black, dome-shaped rock can be reasonably called the Sickness Withdrawal Stone. One bends over it with stomach pressing against its apex, in a "jacknifing" fashion, and lets loose some spittle. If one vomits, all the better, for it is a sign of having been fully purged of illness and, by extension, one's psychospiritual defilements.

Suddenly, we are back in the wounded but reviving precincts of the Place of Joy. And as there is no real beginning nor end in the great circle of absolute reality, our pilgrimage to Ganden *gompa* reaches its end at the first and most accessible building along the road entering the monastery. It is a modest version of the classic temple: two storeys, each with spaces devoted to various divinities, including protectors and fiercer deities who have their own *gönkhang* or Protector's House. There are also a private room, with an unused throne, awaiting the return of the Dalai Lama, and a chanting hall devoted to a variety of buddhas and bodhisattvas who are invoked at frequent ceremonies.

Our party makes the rounds of the shrine rooms, leaving money, prayers and melted butter that is spooned and poured into huge *chömey*, butterlamps, which set the rooms aglow with their warm but eerily flickering light.

And our spirits melt too, like the butter, into a state of being as ancient as these people are to their vast mountainscape. We have become fused with the essence of the place and its divine beings.

And I, for one, have caught the flicker of the feathers of the paradisic phoenix, rising within the shell of the monastery called the Place of Joy. As it lifts into the infinity of the sky, the spirit of this pilgrim is carried along with it.

University of the Spirit

Universities are supposed to be places where the universe is questioned, contemplated and explored with that greatest of spaceships, the human mind.

In the West, universities all too often explore non-universes. Their scholars and researchers are generally straight-jacketed to conceptions of self and existence that have been established through "proofs" derived solely on the physical, material plane.

Today, I am attending a true university, one which explores that infinite universe which can only exist within the limitless precincts of the mind.

Welcome to the University of the Spirit, at Sera Monastery.

Sera Gompa sits silently below arid mountains, a few kilometers from the bustling streets of Lhasa. Its stone buildings are as old as the hills, as is its perennial philosophy: an harmonious fusion of the best of earthly wisdom -the aboriginal awareness of pre-Buddhist Tibet—with that of Buddhism, the science of mind distilled out of twenty-five centuries of effort by the best minds in Asia.

Today, at this renewing monastery, I am witnessing the reflowering of a tradition of inquiry into the fundamental foundations of the mind and, ultimately, reality.

The monks are engrossed in metaphysical debate done in the distinctive Tibetan manner.

Seated on the ground below ancient trees, the small groups of monks proceed with their classes. One among them jumps and postures, parries and thrusts with arms extended, culminating in hands clapping in order to emphasize his question. The answer comes. They argue fervently over such refined topics as the existence or non-existence of phenomena and the nature of mental events. Yet it is as much a ritual dance as an exercise of the intellect.

Old monks question novices; the young question the old, in a quiet garden set aside for the purpose next to the temple of Sera Monastery's Upper College. In the process, they become travelers through space and time. In exploring the diverse realms of mental events, they send out conceptual probes to planets and star systems in shadowy corners of the ultimate universe which is the absolute nature of things—often called the Great Void, in the scientific parlance of Buddhism.

They are explorers into the very nature of reality. Being only human they utilize whatever mental processes are available to them in order to travel into realms beyond ordinary experience.

At times they use deep introspection, through daily meditation, to actually become the object of their speculations, to come to an understanding of how things really are, rather than how they seem.

Just now, amid the din of several simultaneous debating dances, they are using the other tack, that of fiercely incisive logic, to crack a fissure into the Big Question. They cut away improbabilities and impossibilities through the careful scrutiny of dialectical debate. In this technique Westerners come closest to the Tibetan way of inquiry. Beyond this, however, all similarity quickly ends.

For Tibetans always merge the analytical approach with the integrative one of meditative contemplation. It is only then that they begin to see their efforts bear fruit. It is necessary to subject analytical inquiry to the greatest scrutiny of all: the wisdom of the deeper consciousness. No wonder then, that while these seekers of ultimate universal truths are awakening from the fitful slumber of ignorance, we in the West are still dangerously sleepwalking in its grasp.

Still, there remains hope for the enlightenment of this world, so long as the monks of Sera continue to transcend time and space, in the University of the Spirit.

The Monster of Good Fortune

Makara, the crocodile-like sea monster and guardian *extraordinaire* of wealth, health and good fortune, peers down enigmatically at hundreds of monks and laypersons, with bloodshot eyes and a gaping mouth full of wish-fulfilling jewels.

Makara is an elusive but ever present fellow. One encounters him in the most unexpected places. He suddenly materializes out of carved wooden lintels atop colorful pillars in the dark recesses of monastic chanting halls. He glints from the apex of elaborately chased, silver and gold *gahus*, reliquary boxes intended for storing spiritual power-imbued objects. In fact he is apt to be found almost anywhere in the variegated visual environment of Tibet.

Today, however, Makara has come right out into the open. He gazes down, like a ferocious rainbow, from the main, upper panel of a huge tent set up in a meadow beneath Sera Monastery.

This morning, hundreds are assembled for the religious holiday called *chebshu*, a three-day event of ritual offerings and performances beginning with today's activities.

Alternating with their chants and prayers, the monks receive *tsog* offerings in support of their spiritual work. These consist of an unusual abundance of foodstuffs such as sweet rice, oceans of buttered tea and ladles full of thick yogurt. Monk attendants pass from one seated brother to the next dispensing the foods from huge, brass-adorned wooden kettles and bowls.

Behind the main chanting arena of the huge tent, in a tiny canvas alcove dominated by a colorful appliqué array of the eight auspicious symbols, sits a huge Tibetan version of the Shell of Cornucopia, a festively painted *che mar* offering box.

One finds it at most auspicious holidays and ceremonies. But its presence is particularly appropriate today. In the right hand compartment protrudes a healthy pile of recently harvested *dru*, barley kernels. And laying lazily across it, several slabs of butter.

In the left hand compartment, sits a conical pile of the essential product of the harvest, *tsampa*, roasted barley flour, the staple of the Tibetan diet. Then more butter, a critical staple in itself.

Protruding, as if growing from the two piles of barley, are many fat, luscious, healthy and, therefore auspicious, full ears of barley—big as small maize—from the same harvest as that of the kernels and tsampa.

Finally, each compartment sports a *tsebdro*, a vertical plaque decorated with tiny and very finely sculpted flowers and a scene showing the god of old age and good fortune as an ancient, white-haired sage surrounded by his pet deer.

Clearly this entire event is geared toward the perpetuation of good fortune.

Makara, the monster of good fortune must certainly be pleased by all he sees. At least, this is the hope of those gathered here beneath his gaily colored tent, as it's bathed in the incense of smoldering juniper boughs, beneath an ancient monastery and rugged sacred mountains ringing a valley called Place of the Gods, atop the Altar of the Earth.

To Great Heights

Towering Khembu Utse Mountain, the sacred summit dominating a wall of the Lhasa Valley, has seen many of them come and go.

Into its rocks and grass was built one of the world's great communal experiments in living and in pursuing the path toward spiritual perfection.

To call Drepung a monastery would describe its basic purpose. To call it a City of the Spirit would be more to the point.

At the height of its fluorescence, Drepung was home to approximately ten thousand monks, making it the largest monastery in the world at the time, perhaps in all time. Its fields, orchards and herds made it an important economic force in Central Tibetan life. And its role in training *geshes*, the learned Doctors of Divinity of *Vajrayana* Buddhism—as well as its having been a primary place for training the young Dalai Lamas—had made it most influential in matters of spirit and state.

Possessed as it was of a high degree of influence and wealth (of the spiritual as well as the material kind) it seems only right that it is situated in a mountainous niche high above the valley floor.

Just now, outside the *tsuglhakhang chenpo*, the great assembly hall of Drepung, I am treated to a commanding view of that valley called the Place of the Gods. And I am vividly reminded of how significant a quality is height in the lives and thoughts of the Tibetan people.

The heights are dwelling places of ideal beings, the divinities. Generally speaking, the higher their summits (and by extension, the more massive the mountainous foundations for their glorious temple-palaces) the more powerful their teachings and important their status.

Height is also a potent metaphor for the upper reaches that are potential within one's own consciousness—the realm toward which one strives on the path to enlightenment. When one contemplates a mountain's pinnacle, its rarified atmosphere and dissolution from a point into infinity, it becomes a vivid reminder of the process that occurs within when one follows the *nangpa* (inner being) path of Buddhism.

And the heights equally signify a style of living, especially in the case of the monastery. The Tibetan name for monastery is *gompa*, literally meaning a "solitary place." While the *gompa's* solace can be equally found in deserts and in deep forests, the preferred locations in Tibet for places of inner enrichment and retreat are the mountains.

Perhaps it has something to do with the motivational benefits derived from the arduous uphill trek to solitary mountain places. Perhaps too it's the longsighted, infinity view. Mental myopia comes from habitually taking the nearsighted view of reality. But to be constantly surrounded by the distant view puts things into valuable perspective. It allows the mind to observe the relationships among things, to gain that wisdom only derived from seeing the Big Picture.

I suspect, as I sit here in this vast monastic city nestled partway up a sacred mountain, overlooking the Place of the Gods, on the Altar of the Earth, that its very location had much to do with its importance in Tibet's sacred and secular matters.

Attaining great heights obviously contributes to the same.

Compensation

The nineteenth-century philosopher Ralph Waldo Emerson once remarked that in everything there is compensation. For every loss there is a gain and vice versa. It is this way in thoughts and human affairs, as well as in nature.

Take Nechung *gompa* as an example. It sits unassumingly at the base of Khembu Utse Mountain and seems, to uninformed eyes, as merely a "kid brother" to the much larger Drepung Monastery, which hovers above it, further up the sacred mountainside.

But comparisons can be deceiving, especially with respect to these monasteries. Although Drepung appears the more influential of the two, compensation affects how they relate to one another and to the harsh reality of today's Tibet.

Whereas, in the past, Drepung had been a major seat of learning and a beehive of activity, it is today a shell of its former self. Six thousand monks, in residence in 1959, have dwindled to about four hundred souls.

At Nechung *gompa* things, likewise, have not been easy. Countless spiritual relics, treasures and artworks were smashed and stolen during the terror-filled years of the cultural revolution, so much so that, while Drepung was spared major physical destruction, Nechung had been almost reduced to a ruin.

Still, while the physical basis may be severely damaged, that of the spirit often prevails. So while that quality which is Drepung is presently a dormant seed, Nechung *gompa*—the harder hit of the pair—is coming forcefully back to life. The younger monastic brother stirs with the energy of compensation.

All of Nechung's statues are newly made. They appear old, not out of deliberate intent, but because their artists have done their best in the ancient style.

In the western *lhakhang* or "god's house," stand newly made statues of the Nechung Oracle. This monastery had been the home or "seat" of a monk who becomes the *kuten* or "body basis" of the mind energy of a fierce protector divinity named Pehar. The Nechung Oracle—now in residence at the new Nechung *gompa*, in the Tibetan exile community of Dharamsala, India—is the primary source of divinatory advice to the Dalai Lamas concerning the future course of the Tibetan state.

In the eastern chapel two more statues have newly resumed their rightful place in this important temple of the Nyingma sect. Here is Nyima Shonnu Lhamo, the beautiful, red-skinned "Rising Sun Goddess." And there, Palden Lhamo Remati. Her fierce, fanged, blue-black features glower down upon enemies of the religion and upon mental obscurations to our enlightenment.

Between the two chapels stands a *lhakhang* to the Jo Rinpoche—the shrine of Sakyamuni Buddha visualized in his more refined, "adorned" tantric form. Unfortunately the experience of this Jo Rinpoche must be left to the imagination for the time being, since his glorious statue and those of its associated bodhisattvas and protectors have yet to be replaced. Smashed, lotus-shaped pedestals are all that remain.

Throughout my tour I have been in the able hands of Dawa, an eight-year-old boy who has befriended me and is skillfully guiding me around the temple (actually dragging me from one shrine room to the next as if I were a younger sibling!).

Beckoning energetically, he conducts me up to the second

and third storeys of the temple, whose rooms open onto its rooftops. There I encounter newly crafted, gilded statues of ancient teachers, of the Buddha himself and of the sect's guiding saint, Padmasambhava or "Guru Rinpoche" (Great Precious Teacher).

Apart from the imposing statues, a distinct energy can be felt in each shrine room, manifesting in the personalities of their attending monks.

In the Nechung Oracle-Pehar *lhakhang*, for instance, the monks are quite firm, rather sarcastic and unyielding to letting me photograph within its precincts. It seems as if they have assumed some of the qualities of Pehar's own mind and actions.

In the room dedicated to the female protectors, the opposite holds true. The attending monk, named Gonpo—his name appropriately means protector—is full of love and hospitality despite, or possibly according to, his role as guardian of these statues and sacred objects.

Similarly, upstairs in the Guru Rinpoche *lhakhang*, its young monk possesses a certain degree of sternness and forcefulness, not unlike those qualities attributed to the Great Teacher himself. And I suspect that if you and I were there all day, chanting his praises and visualizing ourselves transforming into his being, we would be changed, as well.

Despite their newness, the statues and their ambiences convey an energy as deep as the psyche and as old as time itself.

Had the *gompa*, its statues and staff been all that I encountered this day, I would have been struck by how well they testify to Uncle Ralph's insight into the natural law of compensation. But there is more to come.

On saying goodbye to my young guide and exiting the *gompa's* courtyard, I encounter a group of young monks at the doorway to their residence. All are over eighteen years of age, some well into their twenties. None are any younger since, as they explain, one cannot officially become a monk until reaching the age of eighteen. Clearly this is a purposeful regulation set up by the authorities in order to dissuade many from joining the clergy.

A long conversation ensues, culminating in the predictable request to "please take our picture and...don't forget to send us a copy." And in the process, I am treated, in the inimitable Tibetan manner, to a long tea and conversation before the photo session begins.

I soon learn that they are students at a very special kind of school. Here is taught the venerable tradition of Buddhist philosophical debate, one which has made Gelug sect monasteries, such as Drepung, famous. Interestingly, while Drepung seems to have suffered the full brunt of the effects of a secular society being forced upon its people, here at Nechung *gompa*, one hundred and fifty young monks are reviving an ancient philosophical art renowned in the former monastery.

"So compensation is indeed in full swing here at Nechung *gompa*," run my thoughts as I pose the seven student monks and their master.

Despite the scythes and sickles of those horrible times into which these monks were born, the seeds have refused to die. Instead, as is evidenced everywhere here, they are beginning to sprout anew. And a *gompa* dedicated to propitiating the fiercer divinities of Tibetan Buddhism has become a peaceful garden for cultivating the flowers of wisdom.

Compensation.

Home of Stone, Hearts of Gold

I suspected that Dralha Lupug Monastery was something special, after being accosted several times in the streets of Lhasa, by its gregarious young monks.

Practicing their English, they would grab my hands, ask the usual polite questions about myself, life and country, then invite me to their monastery which is literally carved into the solid rock of Chakpori, Iron Mountain.

Having intended for weeks to make a pilgrimage to Chakpori, I finally set out in its direction one morning, just as the clouds are clearing from the mountains surrounding the Valley of Lhasa.

Instinctively, I follow a circumambulation alleyway, the kind that one encounters everywhere in Lhasa. On coming around a bend in a rockface covered with incised pictures of divinities and awash in the smoke of *sang* incense, I see Dralha Lupug Monastery suddenly looming up along the flank of Iron Mountain.

It is home to twenty two monks, all but one of whom is of the age of the friendly teenaged novice monk who has become my guide. The young monks, in turn, are guided by a middle-aged lama and teacher into the complexities of monastic life.

This *gompa* is one of the most important holy sites of Tibetan Buddhism. The focal point of the monastery is a sacred cave. Legend has it that the cave originally housed a *lü*, a kind of serpentine spirit that inhabits damp, earthy places. When the Jokhang temple was built in Lhasa, this lü and other earth spirits were compelled to help in the work.

Subsequently, the cave became a place of meditational retreat for the great religious king, Songtsen Gampo, under whose direction the Jokhang was built.

We climb up several flights of steps in order to enter the smooth, black rock cavern whose opening is now shielded by a building and gaily painted doorway. And, in the course of a few seconds, the young monk ushers me into quite another world.

Facing the entrance, in a glass display case, sits a statue of the Jo Rinpoche—Sakyamuni Buddha in his guise as a tantric divinity. This form depicts him as residing in the subtle, "adorned and enjoyment" state of beatitude, experienced by bodhisattvas.

Throughout the grotto, images of other divine beings impinge on the consciousness as the eyes adjust to the dim light. What makes this cave all the more special is that most of its sacred images are said to be *rangchung*, naturally self-arisen, my friend the young monk explains.

"They are not carved by human hands. They arose naturally, out of the solid rock. And they are still doing so. Here's the eleven-headed Chenrezi. Here's Drolma. Here, two snow lions are coming out of the rock. Here is Chana Dorje, patron deity of Chakpori. And there is the head of a fierce protector of our religion, fully formed. Over here are *rangchung* figures of Buddha Sakyamuni and of King Songtsen Gampo and his two queens who helped establish Buddhism in our land. There are images of many other deities, as well."

I'd seen "self-arisen" rock images before, at Pharping, in the Kathmandu Valley. Then, as now, the figures—in the process of manifesting fully from the living rock—had been accentuated by the use of a coloring agent: red in Nepal (owing to the Hindu influence) and here, gold. To Tibetans gold is a color that befits a divine being whose enlightened mind possesses a sun-like radiance.

The young monk has now placed me in the charge of another novice. Despite his age, he is already a skilled master of the shrine and its rituals. Like his older peers in other monasteries, he maintains the sacred space with a dignity that goes well beyond his few short years. He dispenses blessed water into the hands of pilgrims with bowed heads, who are often several generations his senior.

He deftly executes the "golden letter" ritual, in which the name of a deceased family member is written out in gold letters on a strip of red paper. He intones special prayers as he burns the missive on behalf of the deceased's consciousness, in the flame of a silver and gold butterlamp, situated on the altar before the Jo Rinpoche statue.

And I cannot help but marvel at the poise and certainty with which he maintains the shrine's altar to the goddess Palden Lhamo. She embodies the fiercely protective energy that guards over the Lhasa Valley, its Dalai Lamas and their Tibetan state.

And I mull over the fact that the presence here of these two young monks—their adult work at such a young age—is the natural response to that very kind of threat to Tibet's well being toward which Palden Lhamo's energy is now being invoked. One intuitively knows, in fact, that such thoughts and prayers for protection are on the minds and lips of all the pilgrims who pause before her altar, at the back of Songtsen Gampo's cave.

One also knows that the altar's presence in the meditation cave of the king, who had consolidated the Tibetan state twelve centuries ago—holding sway even over the Chinese—makes these prayers even more significant.

Indeed, by this old but youthful monastery's presence on a sacred hill, in the Place of the Gods, atop the Altar of the Earth, the message of the unshakeable urge to renew and revive an ancient path of thinking, feeling and living comes through, unmistakably loud and clear.

And with it, comes a feeling of thankfulness for those young monks on the streets of Lhasa, whose invitation brought me into their home of stone and hearts of gold.

A Protected Place

The buttered tea's warmth is most welcome, especially after a day-long rainstorm here in Lhasa. Somewhat soaked, we seek the shelter of this Nyingma sect's monastery, both for its dryness and because it's one of those smaller, lesser known *gompas*, those which often prove the most interesting and hospitable to Western visitors.

The little *gompa* can be found up a side alley from the *barkhor*, the bazaar and circumambulation path around the Jokhang temple, where it is protected from the hustle and bustle of the world-at-large.

Besides being insulated from the world by its hard to find location, it is protected from within by a collection of statues of fierce-looking protector divinities. They stand guard around the central statue of Padmasambhava, the sect's founder. They include, in fact, fierce "emanations"—extrusions of the mind energy—of Padmasambhava himself. The latter are five in number; one dwelling in each of the four cardinal directions and a fifth, the distillation of all their energies, residing at the center of their thus-formed *mandala*.

One also encounters Tamdrin or Hayagriva, the "horse-crowned" tantric protector divinity, as well as the red-skinned,

Nyima Shonnu Lhamo, the Rising Sun Goddess whose beautiful features nonetheless bear a hint of underlying fierceness.

The Nyingmapas are the most earthy and explicitly dramatic of the Tibetan Buddhist sects. Their imagery and ritual services reflect the almost limitless potential of the fertile Tibetan imagination. The style and some of the qualities of their fierce-faced protectors are vivid extrapolations from a population of pre-Buddhist divinities who, in turn, are the essence of the land and the archetypal mental landscape of the native people on the Tibetan Plateau.

The powerful qualities issuing from these statues are quite understandable, considering that the Nyingmapas are masters at dispelling obstacles to one's physical and mental well-being.

Are you, by chance, ill? Then, a ghost dispersal ceremony can be performed by these monks. Have you any deeply ingrained mental impediments to enlightened thoughts? Well, the fierce looking beings, whose energy permeates this colorfully decorated *gompa*, are here to serve your needs with their active powers.

Likewise, the cordial monks, nuns and laypersons who filter in and out of the monastery's temple are here to serve all sentient beings by maintaining a home for the power and wisdom of these divinities.

Muru Nyingba *gompa's* influence extends from the back alleyways of Lhasa to the protectors' fiery realms on the edge of the great Universal Mandala. May it continue to be a protected place as it works for the enlightenment of us all.

The Dalai Lamas

Theocratic Lamentations

The Potala Palace of the Dalai Lamas rises above the valley floor with great majesty. Its form is tempered only by a higher natural law that resides in the proportions of Marpori, the great hill out from which it grows.

As I write these words, I am chewing pieces of *qiaokeli*, the Chinese name for chocolate. Suddenly, I become conscious of two cultures: Tibet, and that which gave the world chocolate, or rather *chocolatl*, the Aztec civilization of ancient Mexico.

The similarities between the two cultures and their ultimate fates are quite remarkable.

Chocolate was the favorite snack (actually, drink) of Motecutzoma (Montezuma), the last God King of the Aztecs. Like his predecessors, he was not only head of a glorious indigenous state, he was a direct link with the gods, possessing divine qualities himself.

His society was a colorful and celebratory one, founded upon religiosity. Its pageants, rituals, dances, songs and inspired visual arts were dedicated to vast pantheons of divinities, in whose qualities was embodied the totality of Aztec reality.

Religious activities centered upon great stone structures, built to reach high into the sky, the realm of the gods. Temples were, accordingly, situated on the summits of these massive pyramids.

The greatest of all these spiritual axes—its base to be precise—was recently uncovered under Spanish colonial buildings. Atop it had been shrines to two divinities: one fierce and warlike, the other fertile and nurturing. They vividly expressed the unification of the fundamentally opposite energies of our perceived world.

Surrounding the pyramid-dominated ceremonial center were vast marketplaces that bustled with activity. It was all to be found within the sacred city called Tenochtitlan, situated in a vast valley ringed with peaks, atop the highest plateau in Middle America which was renamed by its heartless and greedy conquerors: Mexico City.

And conquer the Spanish did. Not only did they scoop up all the gold, silver and precious stones, such as turquoise, that could be found, they tried to and in many cases succeeded in altering the minds of the people by the most powerful sword of all, an uncompassionate brand of European religion.

That happened five centuries ago, at a time during which the world had little knowledge or care for those they considered to be less than human.

The Spanish were doing what all European nations were doing at the time—perhaps just a little more ruthlessly and effectively. In so doing, they wiped from the face of the earth a venerable civilization with roots going back to the dawn of humankind.

Suddenly, all thoughts return to the present time and place. In this mountain encircled valley, on the highest of the world's plateaus, there rises another great monument to the heights of spirituality, embodied in another divine leader.

The Potala Palace possesses a decidedly pyramidal quality. Four-sided and upwardly jutting, it is built on the already high base of Marpori, Red Mountain. Like the Great Pyramid, presided over by Motecutzoma, it too is a place of special sanctity, which is clearly evident in the scores of statues and relics in its butterlamp-lit shrines. Like the Great Pyramid, it too yearns for the infinity of the sky, and all that this implies.

The Potala Palace is the symbol—much as was the Great Pyramid—of the reign of religion in its land. Not the kind of religion that the West is accustomed to and which, in its most disgusting form, destroyed ancient Mexico, but an integrative religion that is really a philosophy of living in harmony with one another and one's land.

That sometimes a religion can give rise to abuses—even ancient integrative ones such as those of Mexico and Tibet—is an unfortunate shortcoming of its practitioners being human. Still, when the decadent throes of ancient Mexico's state religion, and the complacency of that of pre-1959 Tibet are judged in light of the horrendous abuses of European Catholicism and Chinese Maoism, all serious criticism should and does fall away.

The Spanish brutally destroyed an ancient way of life without the world so much as knowing. The People's Liberation Army and Red Guard almost succeeded in doing so while the world looked the other way.

Thus we arrive at the Tibet of 1986. Most of its high, sacred places lie in ruin or have been utterly eradicated. Its religious community is in diaspora.

Fortunately for the Tibetans, the light of their lives, the incarnate object of their devotion and healthful transference of love and respect, the Dalai Lama, lives on in exile. To the Tibetans' loss and the rest of the world's gain, he has become an important voice of sanity and morality on today's international scene.

Motecutzoma was not so lucky. After precious months of indecision as to how to act in the face of the Spanish advances, he was stoned to death by his own people in the fervor of temporary group psychosis. One can understand his reticence to act, after all who could envision a tide of barbarism so despicable as that which would wash over his land? Add to this the prophesied coming of a white-faced teacher whom he mistook for Cortes and the picture of his indecision comes clearer. Tibet too was marked by a certain reticence to act. How could they imagine what was to come?

Societies such as ancient Mexico and Tibet are in many respects fragile things. They are "place specific" cultures and, when all is said and done, admirably but defenselessly geared toward harmony and balance.

Atop the Great Pyramid sat the shrines to the two forces of nature, growth and decay, brought together in harmony and balance. So too, within the Potala's shrines stand divinities who consist of the physical union of male and female forms, and all the psychospiritual implications they evoke.

Being earth-conscious and people-conscious societies, they were limited by the physical watersheds of mountains and valleys, and the more subtle ones of spirituality and morality. They did not become world-threatening megacultures, such as have arisen in Europe, America and some parts of Asia.

Given the importance of religion, it is quite understandable that both cultures found it advantageous to elevate certain human beings—psychically and physically—to the position of incarnate divinities. Having living links with the infinite was an effective solution to political leadership.

Their systems basically operated well. They were relatively stable ones in which the people provided some tribute in order to maintain the state. But unlike in our system of taxation, they generally did so not ungladly. Tribute was also paid through thought and prayer to their God Kings who served as models for individual people to emulate. Such a system worked toward harmony and stability although, of course, no system is, or ever was perfect—especially the more massive it gets.

Certainly ours—we call it democracy—is by no means perfect. Indeed, is it not predicated upon competition and divisiveness? And is it not, ultimately, based upon the dictatorship of ill-fitting compromise at the lowest common denominator, rather than striving for the highest level of thought and action—the divine way—as manifest in Tibet's and Mexico's God Kings?

Not surprisingly, more than vestiges of the ancient ways still survive in Mexico and Tibet. Their philosophies of living tend to ennoble people and give them inner strength. In Tibet, nine out of ten still appear to be devout Buddhists and mob the foreign visitor with requests for photographs of the Dalai Lama.

Fortunately for human beings, civilizations have a way of being like buried seeds that are incubated by the forest fire's heat, allowing the trees to ultimately prevail.

Still, there is a better way. It's the human way of cultivation. We must continue to sow seeds of peace and harmony among the world's superpowers so that the fires are never begun. Swords into ploughshares; may the Tibets and ancient Mexicos lead the way.

Theocratic thoughts and lamentations atop the Altar of the Earth.

The Hill That Touches Heaven

Except for periodic eddies, produced by the occasional splash of the giant carp, the reflection of the Hill That Touches Heaven can easily be the hill itself. Reflected in the park's pond, too, one can make out the metaphysical qualities of this hill, transformed as it is, by the imagination of millions, into a deity's glorious dwelling.

Rising atop Marpori is the Potala Palace of the Dalai Lamas.

To most of us it is a physical place of great majesty and architectural virtuosity. Until the twentieth century it was, in fact, the world's largest high-rise building, constructed without the use of a single nail.

This is the outer Potala, its grossest manifestation.

To others—the devout and those well trained in the consummate powers of the imagination—it has another identity, a deeper essence. When viewed with eyes and minds transformed, it is a palace of more subtle measure than the stone, mortar, wood, gold and silk composing it. It is a rainbow-colored palace of clear, bright light, surrounded by superlative gardens and forests, as only befits an ideal being such as the bodhisattva Chenrezi who has successively incarnated in our realm as the Dalai Lamas.

To such sensitive eyes, the Potala radiates with a preternatural light to all the realms of this world system, from atop a more subtle Altar of the Earth.

As Chenrezi embodies the highly active, boundlessly compassionate qualities of the fully enlightened mind, it is only fitting that his palace be erected atop a hill which has probably been sacred to Tibetans since well before the advent of Buddhism. The Potala suggests that harmonious fusion of the ancient earth religion of Inner Asia—still important in Tibetan daily life—and the masterful science of mind that is Buddhism.

It's only fitting, too, as a metaphor to enlightenment, situated as it is in this valley called Place of the Gods. Its very form, as a vertical extrusion out of a high valley ringed by mountains to the four directions, is a compelling symbol to those who attempt to attain the buddhas' realms, situated atop Mount Meru, the cosmic peak at the universe's center. For these realms are the ultimate font of clear light energy, the same stuff—the lamas tell us— out of which all mind and matter issue.

It is also a metaphor to the central task at hand in all our lives: that we all possess mental, physical and communicative assets and debits which we have to utilize in our uphill climb toward self-perfection.

Red Mountain Hill rises formidably, in a valley dedicated to the spirit. It is a beacon to all who strive for perfection of themselves and others, in that strangely compelling dance called life.

The Temple Beyond Time

The Fourteenth Dalai Lama has now given the *Tunkhor Wang-chen*, the Kalachakra Tantric Initiation, many times; both in Asia and the West. While many great lamas are empowered to teach this all-encompassing and complex system for the transformation into enlightenment of one's thoughts and physical processes, it is still considered by many to be the special provenance of the Dalai Lamas.

I now understand why, sitting here in the Tunkhor *lhakhang*, the God's House of Kalachakra, Lord of the Cycles Beyond Time.

The teachings and practices of the Kalachakra Tantra had been sustained over the centuries in this chapel, secreted within the Potala Palace. Tradition relates that this tantra came to Tibet from Shambhala, the mystic, pure land of the north, by way of India.

Of the innumerable shrines in this massive temple-palace, the Kalachakra God's House is one of the most important.

Rays of sunlight from a single window set into the Potala's thick stone wall, slice through the otherwise dark room. It is a quiet beacon to pilgrims who enter the chapel from out of a bewildering assortment of balconies and stairwells.

As is the Buddhist custom, they circulate clockwise through the God's House. They pass scores of statues of divinities. Significant among them is the eleven-headed, one thousand-armed Chenrezi, in whose palace, and under whose compassionate patronage the Kalachakra Tantra is preserved and taught.

Continuing around, one comes to the most elaborate and largest gilded statue in the *lhakhang*, the very statue of Kalachakra which the Dalai Lamas themselves would have meditated upon and given offerings.

Like most major tantric tutelary deities, Kalachakra is actually the combination of two divine figures—male and female— symbolizing the union of two essential qualities inherent in the male-like, methodical pursuit of female-borne, enlightened wisdom.

Thus, Kalachakra and Vishvamata—Mother of Diversity— are depicted as "sporting" in sexual union. This signifies the neccessary fusion of those energies that must be called upon from within one's own totality, in order to effect a quick and smooth passage to enlightenment.

The thirty-two arms that they share between them and which hold a variety of symbolic implements, are the sum total of the numerous variables that one learns to master in the course of becoming, through the window of initiation into Kalachakra's mysteries, the child of Kalachakra and Vishvamata.

This is the tantra that teaches about the cyclic nature of the natural universe: the course of the stars, periods of the planets, seasons, days and nights, sun and moon, even historical epochs. It also reveals, on a more intimate level, the ebbs and flows of one's own blood and lymph, even the currents of *chi* energy that surge through the meridians of one's psychic nervous system.

The tantra teaches, too, a way of dealing with all this cyclic diversity, by harnessing one's mind and body to come into harmony with it. This "alternate" path is founded upon the teachings of the divinity, and the purifying empowerment or "initiation" given by the guiding lama in order to practice them.

To think, this venerable wisdom was refined at the very spot on which I stand: between the statue of Kalachakra (interestingly the attending monk never refers to it as a statue, but as the deity itself) and a fantastic sculptured monument.

The latter sits centrally within the chapel, dominating it. One must walk around it to get to the Kalachakra statue and the massive butterlamps that burn incessantly before the huge silver and gold form. It is a material expression of the Universal Temple of Kalachakra called, in Tibetan, *Tunkhor Kyinkhor*, the *mandala* of Kalachakra.

A constant flow of Tibetan pilgrims, and not a few Westerners, stream by it. The Tibetans leave *khatag* offering scarves after a mindful prayer, and add butter to the great lamps — some burning as many as five wicks in the golden magma. They approach the monk attendant who disperses blessed water into their hands, which they drink. They then wipe the remaining drops on the crowns of their heads—seat of the highest quality of consciousness. The Westerners, meanwhile, wander about in dazed awe.

The *mandala* is the embodiment—in this gross, physical plane of relative existence—of Kalachakra's temple at the center of a resplendent universe. In terms of absolute reality, it exists in the realm of mental energy as a phantasm of clear, rainbow-colored light that is best experienced through the powers of the imagination, in visualizations. Indeed, it is only through this door of perception that one can fully appreciate the temple's unique character and its complexity.

Imagine a palatial, five-storied temple, composed entirely of glowing, rainbow-colored light, covered with glittering jewels and surrounded by fragrant gardens. It all floats on lotus-shaped clouds, atop Mount Meru, the metaphysical axis of our universe. Each of its sides has a great portal, opening onto one of the four cardinal directions. This configuration is repeated at two higher levels, so that there are three storeys with four such entranceways in each. These levels are called (starting with the ground floor) the Body *Mandala*, Speech *Mandala* and Mind *Mandala*. Their names refer to the three characteristics which compose a being's totality of actions.

Populating the three levels are a bewildering number of divinities, ranging from fierce guardian protector types at the *mandalas'* edges, to more peaceful and refined ones, deeper within.

Atop the Mind *Mandala* are two higher levels. The fourth floor is the Pristine Consciousness *Mandala*, populated by forms of the five buddhas who are at the root of all tantric systems. The fifth and highest level, the Great Bliss *Mandala*, is the actual abode of Kalachakra.

To complicate matters even further, one realizes that the seven hundred and twenty-two deities residing within Kalachakra's Universal Temple are one and the same with Kalachakra. They all are emanations of that enlightened mindstream of which Kalachakra is the emblem.

So, with the right set of mind, one not only enters the chapel dedicated to Kalachakra, one is transported to a purer state of being within his *mandala*.

Thoughts such as this also arise in scores of other sacred spaces in this massive palace called the Potala. For it is envisioned in a similar manner to the "beehive" temple of Kalachakra. The Dalai Lamas' palace's many chapels, storeys and treasuries of sacred objects suggest the various paths and levels of awareness possible in the world of the spirit.

In the end, the Potala and Kalachakra *lhakhang* are dynamic expressions of the Tibetan way of comprehending reality. It is a reality that exists simultaneously on gross and sublime levels. It is both a world of suffering that is full of great potential and, at the same time, a universe of potential enlightenment full of great bliss.

Kalachakra's tantra is one effective path for attaining this timeless state.

Palace of the Serpent King

Twelve eyes gaze outward over their watery domain. Six *makaras*, crocodile-like sea monsters, stand guard on the golden roof of their master's lovely palace. They look out over a lake to the four cardinal directions and to the zenith and nadir. They bristle with that power which is horded at the lake's bottom, in the form of *norbu*, wish-fulfilling jewels.

These six are denizens of the realm of the Lü Gyalpo, the King of Serpentine Consciousness whose mind power is inherent in this lovely lake, situated directly behind the Potala.

On a tree-covered island at the lake's center sits the tiny palace—some might call it a pavilion—with three colorfully painted storeys, set to the four cardinal directions and crowned by the *makaras'* golden roof.

It is a quiet spot which, despite occasional noise from traffic on the large road outside its park, manages to impart a palpable serenity.

The lake has been important to Tibetans for many centuries. Legend has it that at one time living sacrifices had been made to the Serpent King in order that he continue to provide the bounty of his wish-fulfilling jewels to the people.

Nowadays the offerings are more humane. Tibetans give inanimate but mentally alive offerings to divinities of the earth's watery realms. These *lü* are considered to manifest in physical form as snakes, frogs and scorpions. Visualized inwardly, they appear as mermasters and mermaids with bodies of snakes instead of fish.

Giving offerings to the *lü* continues to be an essential aspect of practical Tibetan spirituality. For just as they can insure health, wealth and happiness, the *lü* can also bring their opposites into one's life.

Nowadays, offerings to the king of these spirits often take the form of prayer flags: rainbow-colored cotton rectangles, strung seemingly haphazardly from tree limb to painted pillar, all about the tiny island paradise.

The colorful offerings are meant as well for other divine beings who, for centuries, too had found pleasure within the palace. Since the time of The Sixth, Dalai Lamas would meditate and relax in its lovely surroundings. They would descend to it from the heights of the Potala Palace in order to listen to the nighttime insects, the rustling leaves and lapping water.

It is said that the island pavilion, called Lü Khang, House of the Serpent King, served the colorful Sixth Dalai Lama as a pleasure palace supreme. He is particularly remembered for his sensual poetry which one may find to contain a good deal of spiritual teachings among its voluptuous syntax.

He is also remembered for behavior suggesting that he was not a celibate Dalai Lama—not that it's necessary to take monastic vows in order to be a Gwalya Rinpoche (the lineage title of Dalai Lamas). Still, custom dictates that the Dalai Lama be a monk, in order to most effectively provide his services to sentient beings as an incarnation of Chenrezi. So his "aberrent" behavior has made some people uncomfortable, over the centuries.

Seen in a different light, it may well have been that he had practiced what he preached. It is said that he used the Lü Khang for private trysts with lovers drawn from among the beauties of Lhasa. Yet one suspects that, in a certain abstrusively symbolic way, his behavior might have been fully in keeping with the psychocosmic qualities of the island palace in the Serpent King's lake, and its relationship with questions of mind and matter.

Let me try to explain.

From the standpoint of geomancy—the universal human teachings on proper spiritual placement of manmade and natural phenomena—this lake, its pavilion and the Potala Palace situated atop the hill behind the lake are exactly and appropriately situated within the Tibetan scheme of things.

Every sacred hill or mountain should have a body of water-referably a lake—below it, according to this view. One form calls up the inherent maleness of mountains and sky; the other embodies the femaleness of the watery realm: male and female in body and spirit. Male and female energies are central, as well, to understanding the processes of mind. According to the tantric lineages of Tibetan Buddhism, a balance between these two energies must be struck within one's own consciousness for enlightenment to occur.

So, in a strange way—and strange ways are readily understandable to Tibetans when such ways are possessed by omniscient, living buddhas such as Dalai Lamas—the Sixth Dalai Lama's dalliances seem completely appropriate to the setting.

One can imagine how he would come down from the sundrenched rocky heights of the Potala into the moonlit coolness of the palace within its oval body of water. There, the human expressions of these environmental and psychological phenomena would be physically joined.

Psychospiritual yogic practice, or purely passion? Who knows? And, does it ultimately matter? The Tibetans certainly don't seem to worry over the enigma. For the lake, its tiny palace and its inhabitants are beyond mere physical objects. Their significance lies on a much more subtle plane.

At Leisure in the Jeweled Garden

First come the smiles then an exclamation of *alé!*, at the sight of my left hand busily scrawling out these words. I sit with a Tibetan family on colorful woolen carpets under an old shade tree. We are in the preeminent picnic place of Lhasa, the Norbu Lingka, or Jeweled Garden, which surrounds the summer palaces of several Dalai Lamas.

Little Jigme is having a fine time, just now, leaning on my knee. A number 120 film spool dangles from his mouth, while his family partakes of the cool leisure of the garden.

Tashi, my Tibetan friend from Kathmandu, informs the family that is offering us their hospitality, of the latest events among the Tibetans in exile.

Two sisters, dressed in the fashion of Lhasa's young women—bellbottom pants and hip hugging sports jackets—serve up interminable cups of buttered tea.

The family's modest pavilion, defined by broad strips of cloth strung from the trunks of trees into an enclosed square area, repeats a custom as old as the hills surrounding the Jeweled Garden.

As soon as summer arrives, Tibetans renew their ancient nomadic roots by picnicking and camping in a pleasant natural place. Some groups spend weeks in their colorful tents, wherever a nice park or field may present itself. Many who pitch their tents in the Jeweled Garden wait to do so until the lunar month of July/August when carnival, "Tibetan style" takes place. The holiday's name is *shötun* and it is the celebratory apex of the summer for Lhasaites, and their relatives and friends who have come from afar on religious and secular business.

It is the time for performances of Tibetan operas in the Jeweled Garden. They tell graphic tales from ancient times. Their elaborate plots, colorful masks and costumes, dances and songs help the pressing crowds travel to another time, place and reality, well beyond the opera arena's huge tent.

Songs, too, are sung by almost everyone who comes to these tree-shaded grounds for family conviviality, gambling, foods, buttered tea and inebriating draughts of *chang*.

As in the old days, a picnicker may bring out a *damnyen*, the banjo-lute of Tibet, and begin a friendly sing-along of the lovely old songs for which Lhasa is justly famous.

Song after song fills the airways, along with the chatter of adults, screams of children and the percussive tap-slapping of the gambling games, *sho* and *mahjong*.

This is an amusement park without the noisesome mechanical contrivances with which we litter our pleasure gardens in the West.

Today the Norbu Lingka is a pleasure garden for the people-at-large. But it is, first and foremost, a pleasure garden for a particular deity, the bodhisattva known as Chenrezi, who embodies the boundlessly compassionate aspect of the enlightened mind field which is Buddha.

Chenrezi—symbolized in his "active" aspect of eleven heads and one thousand arms that radiate in all directions— further emanates into the line of successive Gwalya Rinpoches, better known to the world as the Dalai Lamas. The Norbu Lingka has been the site of their summer retreats since the reign of the Seventh Dalai Lama, during the eighteenth century.

Sitting here among the endless flowers and varied types of

trees that adorn wide, flagstone promenades and elaborately decorated palaces, one can appreciate how it was conceived of as a pleasure garden more for a deity than a human being.

Summer palaces of the Seventh and Thirteenth Dalai Lamas stand amid their own walled-in gardens. But the focal point of the Norbu Lingka is the preserved palace of the present, Fourteenth Dalai Lama, completed during his short rule, in 1956.

That the Dalai Lamas should have their own palaces and garden is hardly an example of Asiatic excess, as has often been asserted by humorless and colorless political critics. It is rather a matter of a spiritual imperative central to the Tibetan mind.

According to the *Mahayana* Buddhist way of seeing things, we are all reincarnated consciousnesses. A very few, however, are different from the others in a significant way. They have attained great mental clarity and compassion, having reached—within their lifetimes—a state of omniscience called buddhahood. Although their liberated consciousnesses could take freedom from the future rebirths that plague the rest of us, they choose to return, in human form, from one generation to the next. They do so according to the Bodhisattva Ideal—a fundamental in this form of Buddhism—of helping all other beings attain a state of liberation from psychophysical suffering, and entry into omniscience of the absolute nature of things.

So, it is for one of these bodhisattvas, incarnate in successive Dalai Lamas, that these pleasure palaces have been built here in the Jeweled Garden. Compared with the grotesque and scandalously opulent retreats of heads of state in the modern world—be it East or West—the Norbu Lingka is utterly simple, yet sublime.

Its few gilded and jeweled thrones and altar objects, its buildings' tasteful architectural forms and the long stone promenades, are not so much expressions of material worth as they are of spiritual and philosophical wealth. As such, they serve as valuable models for creating a quality environment in the *mandala* of each of our own lives.

In the end, when the Tibetan people come to picnic and

sing, feast and gamble, to reverently shuffle through the Fourteenth Dalai Lama's rooms, to prostrate and give offerings before his bed and throne, they are tapping into that jewel-like realm that glows within the pleasure gardens of their own minds.

The People

1. The golden roofs of the Jokhang—holiest temple in Tibet— tower over Lhasa ("Place of the Gods") as do sacred mountains tower over the Kyichu ("Waters of Happiness") River Valley in which the town and temple sit. (Tour de Force in the House of the Lord)

2. All of Tibet congeals along the *barkhor*, the circular roadway, market and pilgrim path around the holy Jokhang Temple in Lhasa. Here, two Khampa girls from Derge take time out from a busy day of selling turquoise, coral and trinkets to passersby. (Circling the House of Mysteries)

3. The Kumbum Chörten at Paljor Chöde Monastery in Gyangtse, is a grand physical expression of the *mandala* universe of Dorje Chang, the Primordial Buddha. Climbing through numerous galleries of images of divinities, and up into its cupola, provides pilgrims with a vivid experience of the ascent that ultimately must be made with the mind. (One Hundred Thousand Paths to a Buddha)

4. The monks of Tashilungpo Monastery, in Shigatse, proceed to the "debating garden" for the final stages of a four-day-long ceremony. They will give offerings to the "obstacles," ghosts and demons who would cause illness or harm to befall their beloved abbot, the Panchen Rinpoche. (A Stitch in Time)

5. The Yarlung Tsangpo River, highest major river system on earth and lifeline of Central Tibet, glistens in the early evening light. Prayer flags flutter atop holy Haibori Hill, testifying to the sacredness of this place and the ancient Samye Monastery, spreading behind and below it. (At the Crossroads)

6. The Potala Palace, situated atop Lhasa's sacred Marpori Hill, is the primary dwelling of the Dalai Lamas. It is also considered the outer expression of the palace of Chenrezi, *bodhisattva* of compassion, whom the Dalai Lama incarnates. (The Hill that Touches Heaven)

7. In this isolated valley, agriculture, the first dynasty of kings and the fundamental pattern of Tibetan civilization have all arisen. Yet being there still brings great solace and quietude to the mind. (Silence, Solace and Solitude)

8. The now empty Potala Palace—one of the architectural wonders of the world—was built by and for Tibet's divine leaders, the Dalai Lamas. They ruled through a partnership of religion and statesmanship, in a political system that proved to be too fragile for a heartless, contemporary world. (Theocratic Lamentations)

9. A student monk at Sera Monastery challenges his teacher, in the vital traditional manner, with a question of Buddhist dialectical philosophy. (University of the Spirit)

10. Like this nomad family from Northeastern Tibet, pilgrims come to Lhasa from the farthest reaches of the Altar of the Earth to be blessed by the holy objects and ambience of the Jokhang Temple. But their religious work doesn't preclude enjoyable business dealings in the *barkhor* bazaar, located around the Jokhang. (Circling the House of Mysteries)

11. The highest peaks on earth seem only modest mountains from 17,400 foot Lakpa-la Pass. But to the people living on their northern slopes, the Himalayas are palaces of divinities who nurture the Tibetans and protect their religion. In the end, the mountains are metaphors for the upward urge toward enlightenment in us all. (Altars of the Earth)

12. Samye Monastery is a focus of every pilgrimage to Central Tibet. Its inner courtyard encircles a chanting hall and temple. Here pilgrims spin numerous prayer wheels, which bear within them invocations to deities, and also vocalize these mantras on behalf of the enlightenment of themselves and all beings. The more mantras chanted or spewn out from the whirling prayer wheels, the more quickly the advent of enlightenment for all. (At the Crossroads)

13. Samye Monastery is more than the oldest monastery in Tibet. It is an architectural rendering of the metaphysical cosmos. Mount Meru, its central sacred peak, is embodied in the temple and chanting hall, while the four world continents and the sun and moon are symbolized by various outer buildings and monuments. (At the Crossroads)

14. Nomad *ngagpas* (tantric masters—magicians) from Nagchu are on pilgrimage at Yumbulhakhang. Traditionally considered the castle of Tibet's first kings—since the supernatural king Nyatri Tsenpo came down from the sky at the end of a cord of rainbow light—it had stood intact until its destruction during the cultural revolution. It was rebuilt a few years ago in the original manner. (The Rainbow Path from the Sky)

15. The present, XIV Dalai of Tibet enjoyed only three years of retreat in his summer palace at the Norbu Lingka—the "Jeweled Garden"—on the outskirts of Lhasa. Today, Tibetans come from afar to pay their respects and enjoy its tree-shaded grounds. (At Leisure in the Jeweled Garden)

16. The Jokhang Temple, built by King Songtsen Gampo and Queen Bhkruti Devi, is situated on the site of a sacred lake, set into the "Milky Plain," in the heart of Lhasa, Place of the Gods. Day and night, pilgrims prostrate and pray with great devotion before its huge doors. (Tour de Force in the House of the Lord)

17. Ganden Monastery, the "Solitary Place of Joy," suffered a most horrible fate after China's annexation of Tibet. After having been totally destroyed by explosives and artillery, it is being rebuilt by Tibetan voluntary labor and contributions. In its revival—like the legendary phoenix from the fire's ashes— Ganden now serves as a potent symbol of the Tibetans' will to survive and to continue their spiritual quest for the enlightenment of all beings. (Phoenix from the Ashes)

18. A field of barley stands ready for harvesting in Samye Village. Towering over it stands sacred Haibori Hill, atop which sits a shrine to buddhas, and to aboriginal divinities of the earth under whose influence the barley grows. (At the Crossroads and The First Field of Tibet)

19. A pilgrim has traveled many miles and weeks to offer respects to his deities and their teachings. He prostrates fully before the main doors of the temple at Samye Monastery. (At the Crossroads)

20. Daily, pilgrims give offerings to the full range of divinities—Buddhist and aboriginal—
that influence the course of their lives. The offering of burnt fragrances—using juniper
incense, called *sang*—is the time-honored method. Buy a bale of *sang* on the *barkhor*
market road in Lhasa then offer up its smoke at a convenient streetside censer. (Circling
the House of Mysteries)

21. Nomad women and children—along with their menfolk—have made a long pilgrimage to Samye Monastery from the green hills and plains of Amdo, the northeastern reaches of Tibet. The women's one hundred and eight braids—swathed with yak butter—reflect the sacredness of this number in Buddhist ritual and philosophy. (At the Crossroads)

22. The author at *Lake Yamdrok Tso*. *Yamdrok Tso*, a great turquoise lake—at fourteen thousand feet in Central Tibet—is a place of pure waters and great solace. Meditators have found in its reflections deep inspiration. (The Lake of Clear Light) This photograph is by Marcie Rothman. All other photographs are by Peter Gold.

Khampas On Wheels

Their fields and steppes are now city streets. Their horses, made from aluminum and steel. The landscape and means of horsepower have changed but the same red and black silk strands still fly from their jet black hair as they hurtle along.

Look out, the Khampas now have "wheels."

You can see them everywhere, nowadays, on Chinese built bicycles, barreling down the narrow cobbled lanes and back alleyways of Old Lhasa.

You can find them too at rest, congregating in front of the Jokhang temple, leaning against their bikes as they do their horses back in Kham, the easternmost reaches of Tibet.

In between frenetic bursts of speed they find time for gossiping and trading trinkets of all kinds. Some of their wares are old, some new, some newly made to look old.

Sometimes the urge to do business calls from afar then, suddenly, these colorful and clever men leap onto their nether steeds, as if rearing Tibetan ponies, and careen their way along the impossibly crowded *barkhor*, the market and pilgrimage street around Tibet's holiest shrine.

If you have ever found yourself in the path of a Khampa biker then you surely will have known what fear is. For the

Khampas are a fearless lot. Their horse-borne guerilla warfare against the Chinese army—during the early years after its invasion of Tibet—is legendary. Find yourself in their path and you will know the wanton spirit of those considered to be the "wild bucks" of Tibet.

Bicycles are hardly horses, and rather less dignified when ridden. Also they render the rider most vulnerable. As such, they make the men of Kham, with their proud faces, flowing headdresses and prominently displayed, long daggers seem ill-itted to these latter day horses.

But, as of late, things have begun to take a new and—if you are a Khampa—exciting turn in their world of biking. Just the other night I had been walking along the normally placid back streets of Banak Shöl, an old Lhasa neighborhood, when its roar preceded a motorcycle around a sharp curve in the narrow alleyway. Even before I was able to discern much of the motorcycle's details I caught the indelible flash of its Khampa rider's red silk hair sash.

It seemed as if the wheel of world history had noticeably turned another notch, in time with the Honda's spoked wheels.

Khampas are obviously beginning to trade in their bicycles for bikes more suited to their temperaments and their rakish lifestyle.

No doubt, the streets of Lhasa will soon be filled with their distinctive warrior cries above the roar of Japanese motorcycles. And when that happens, God help the pedestrian!

In the meantime, enjoy your stroll along the fascinating streets of Lhasa. But keep one eye open for a flash of red or black silk and a careening bicycle.

Remember, the Khampas now have wheels!

Playing

I

They bob and swoop then smoothly glide below Bumpari, the Sacred Water Vase Peak.

They seem so happy, these red, blue and purple paper kites, masterfully wielded by Tibetan boys in the airways above the Lhasa Valley.

It's kite flying time in Tibet. There's hardly a more exciting pastime for a Tibetan boy than that which lets him touch the sky—actually enter into the realm of the gods—with a single, thin thread attached to a kite of his own making.

With the flick of a wrist he can send up thoughts and watch them dance and dive in buddha fields—those invisible sky-high paradises reserved for the pleasure of enlightened beings. Perhaps one day his own *sem*, his consciousness (which, the lamas tell him, transfers from one "body basis" to another—we call them incarnations), will join the Enlightened Ones who have defeated the gravity and inertia of suffering and illusion.

Wherever one looks in Tibet the people are celebrating height. For Tibetans, height is synonymous with the upward urge toward self-realization. To climb a mountain "because it's there" is a ludicrous idea, unless it is to plant a prayer flag or burn juniper incense at its summit, requesting the mountain god's or buddhas' benevolence and qualities of mind.

Tibetan stories and religious teachings are full of references to rainbow cords coming down from the sky, linking beings up with its infinity. What better physical metaphor to the striving for perfection of one's mental heights than a brightly colored flag at the end of an all but invisible kite string?

II

The boys grow older and kites give way to more pressing concerns. Fathering and surviving take precedence—as they do worldwide—to boyhood's revels.

Still, when life is hard people play hard. Playing gives an outlet from the harsh realities of living. For the Tibetan man it manifests in gambling, fueled by liberal helpings of the potent grain beer, *chang*.

Strange as it may seem, modest gambling—like the kite—is but another conduit to the world of the spirit.

Let me explain.

When Tibetan men play their dice game called *sho*, they set their minds and fates squarely upon a flying horse that bears jewels of wish fulfillment on its saddle.

The Wind Horse, *lungta*, is a commonly encountered symbol. It is often seen on prayer flags, which are referred to by the name *lungta* when the Wind Horse's picture is printed by woodblock at the flag's center.

The *lungtas* also bear *mantras*, invocations and prayers to invoke the qualities of mind, expression and action of buddhas, as well as to bring health, wealth and good luck to all beings with each flap in the wind.

So, what does a spiritual Pegasus have to do with gambling —or kites, for that matter?

Well, for the most part, Tibetan men gamble solely according to what we would call chance. They call it luck or *lungta*.

"Oh, my *lungta* is high today," explains a Tibetan who has just experienced a good turn of events. His luck is high, like the high flying horse and prayer flags which bear the same name.

Likewise, one may also hear: "my *lungta* is low today," that is to say, "things don't go too well."

So when the men play their animated games of *sho*, they set themselves squarely upon the saddle of the *lungta*, to rise and fall with its precious cargo of wish-fulfilling jewels, which are the measure of their fortunes at that very moment.

With the throw of the dice they open their beings' wings to the winds of karma, relying on the effects of past actions to "ripen" into a win or a lose.

Tibetan boys send up their kites and thoughts into the brisk wind blowing atop the Altar of the Earth and become one with the infinity of the heights. They trust the kite and wind to bring them there.

When they get older they send their thoughts upward on the wings of another kind of wind device, likened to a flying horse. They mount the Wind Horse too through games of chance which are, in the end, indicators of the rise and fall of the wind horse of wish fulfillment and luck, which carries them through life.

Life's a game, after all, and Tibetans generally live out life's dramas with a distinct light heartedness. And, in the end, isn't attaining this state of ease in one's thoughts, expressions and actions the true purpose of being at play?

Circling the House of Mysteries:
An Evening Along the Barkhor in Lhasa

House of the Mysteries,
inner sanctum of the Place of the Gods,
glints like a golden pleasure dome
on a mountaintop divine;

Day and night they come
to prostrate and pray;
to turn prayer wheels large and small;
to be close to the holiest shrine of all.
Meanwhile horns and chants and drums and prayers
rebound unceasingly from within their temple home;

The steady stream of pilgrims
passes like an endless river,
a clockwise, sunwise flow of humanity—
part devotional, part evening constitutional—
around the Jokhang's sacred core;

Prostrators with booming voices,
spread out full-bodied,
giving their all to the power divine,
without them, and within;

A poor nun, like so many
before her and still to come,
"Dalai Lama's photo please," she begs of me,
then another approaches and all I can say is
"sorry, I truly haven't one with me:"
truth sometimes hurts severely;

Ngagpa, master of the tantric path
and powers over darkness,
chants with bell and double drum
day in and day out.
For his intense concentration
and concerned intentions,
the devoted leave a modest reward;

Butter, soot and body-oiled pilgrims
from faraway villages and nomadic camps,
sit eating, resting, prayer wheels spinning,
sleeping and gossiping, nursing and grinning;

Interminable stalls of everything
one needs or doesn't need at all,
a true bazaar in the old world way
amid a flood of pilgrims;

An avalanche of trinkets:
some old, some new, some newly made old;
prayer wheels, daggers, sunglasses, saddles,
vases, rugs, dresses, aprons, sashes,
rings and coins, prayer beads and prayer flags,
vegetables, fruits, household goods,
bales of mountain sheep's wool...
It's endless!

Senses are satiated in an ancient human manner,
through sights and smells, tastes and feels,
but especially in the sounds.
Old men chat to tapping walking sticks;
young monks chant to bells and prayer texts;
a pilgrim dances, sings and fiddles for his meal;

Rows of *sang* bales
—juniper incense—
burn it in the brazier behind you;
comes a manifold spiritual return.
Smoke billowing everywhere,
almost obscuring
bright-colored carpets
hanging nearby;

Red and black silk threads
dangle in jet black hair;
proud faces, clever glances,
Khampa men strong as their daggers,
line up like toadstools
on ledges along the circular roadway;

Boys carefully concentrate,
pulling on spools of invisible thread,
turn high-flying kites into paper hawks diving,
in a sky of a clear lapis blue;

Unfortunate pilgrim man,
nyumba, a "crazy one,"
knocks his head against an ancient stone pillar
in view of the holy temple.
Does his grief—his pain—come from sadness,
or a strangely felt sense of relief?

Nomad girls in homespun rainbows
walk the *barkhor* hand in hand.
There, a village mother—tired but happy,
with child strapped to her back
in American Indian fashion;

Like threads embroidered later
into a colorful tapestry
of motions and forms,
beggars—everywhere—gesticulate wildly;

Pilgrims pause to watch
this long-nosed stranger,
scribbling out these very words.
His unsanitary left hand
flinging out phrases like excretia;

Chinese strollers, unwanted settlers,
uncommunicative in dark sunglasses,
Walk the wrong way round the House of Mysteries.
Don't they know the results of their actions?

Clumps of occidental tourists,
like their colonial ancestors,
know only that they must get here;
wade bewildered through this human sea,
awestruck and shipwrecked;

Around and around, like a great wheel spinning,
like the cycles of the seasons,
days and nights they are walking;
like the cycles of lifetimes,
timeless journeys,
no beginnings,
but somewhere find their ending.

Place of the Gods

Place of the Gods

Lhasa,"Place of the Gods;" I think I finally understand the name, as I scan this massive valley from my vantage point astride the sacred mountain Bumpari.

From here, the Lhasa valley—cut eons ago by the Kyichu River, the Waters of Happiness—spreads out in all its austere beauty. The Kyichu and its glacial ancestors cut a wide swatch through the rugged mountains that enclose this stratospheric land, as if jutting fingers in a cupped and upraised hand.

The Waters of Happiness rush exuberantly today, They are a distinct turquoise green from having been infused into a mineral brew of the rocky flesh of alpine places. And everywhere that the waters meander gravel bars twist and bend in complex harmony with their flow.

Beyond the turquoise river and the arid beige "hills" (actually massive peaks over sixteen thousand feet in height), the sky stretches interminably but with a telltale flatness. It tells us that this is the closest "level" place on earth to the zenith of the dome of air that we offhandedly call the sky.

Now at midday, as at almost every midday the year around, it's all bathed in the sun's luminescence. The solar fire burns here like nowhere else, save the highest peaks directly on the equator.

The world has known several valleys of the sun. Surely Nyima Lhasa, "Sunny Lhasa" as it's fondly called by its inhabitants, is one of them. Snow has little chance here, even in the dead of winter, with a furnace such as this so close at hand.

Here, the primal elements of earth, air, fire and water meet in a dizzying dance. It transmutes them into their ultimate alchemical distillation, the element of space or ether, whose most immediate and personal manifestation is mind.

No wonder, then, that situated high upon the most prominent free-standing hill within this great valley, floats the Potala, the palace of the Dalai Lamas. It is envisioned by the Tibetan inner eye as the temple of the bodhisattva Chenrezi, out of whose enlightened mind energy the Dalai Lamas are said to emanate, and also as the heart of a metaphysical universe or *mandala*.

For hundreds of years, the Dalai Lamas had taught the essence of the five tantric buddha paths from atop sacred Marpori. Each path—having a particular buddha as its emblem—embodies the quality of one of the five primal elements; a color (red, yellow, blue, green or white); a cardinal direction, and the center from which they are reckoned; and an enlightened wisdom whose mastery dispels one of the five root causes of mental and physical afflictions originating from the central one of ignorance.

In this way, four directional buddhas dissolve into a distillation of them all, symbolized by a fifth, all-encompassing buddha. This buddha is envisioned as residing in the center of the five buddhas' *mandala*, a subtle, "metaphysical" temple in a resplendent place atop a cosmic mountain.

This *mandala* view of subtle reality, taught by the Dalai Lamas from their temple at the focal point of the *mandala* of Lhasa,is a central conception upon which the *Vajrayana*, the "Diamond Path" of Tantric Buddhism, is founded.

Sacred Heights

There are three sacred heights in the Lhasa Valley. From each
of the three summits one has an unobstructed view of this most
sacred valley in Tibet.

The three hills are places of particular gods, divinities associated with the three qualities of the Buddha Mind.

One is named Marpori, Red Mountain. Built upon its summit is the Potala Palace, considered a material expression of
the universal temple of the bodhisattva Chenrezi.

Another sacred summit gracing the Place of the Gods is
Chakpori, Iron Mountain. This conical extrusion out of the
valley floor harbors the powerful will and skillful ways and
means of the enlightened mind, envisioned as the fierce-looking
bodhisattva, Chana Dorje.

We can see them clearly from atop Ponpori, the third sacred
hill in the Lhasa Valley. We are at the gate to the Gesar *lhakhang*, a temple named for the epic warrior and folk hero of
old, Gesar of Ling. But the hill itself is dedicated to an even
greater warrior, thundering forth from within the Buddhist
pantheon.

Jambayang (Manjushri) bears a more potent sword than Gesar. His is aflame with the energy that cuts through ignorance.

As such, he is the bodhisattva embodying the transcendental wisdom of the Buddha Mind, that same energy potentially inherent within us all.

Though this temple is physically destitute, a short visit convinces us that Jambayang's qualities are alive and well within its walls. Its degraded condition is the result of years of deliberate destruction and enforced neglect, initiated during the cultural revolution. Its skeletal crew of an old couple serving as caretakers, an elderly monk, two teenaged girls and their lama imparts to the quiet courtyard and destroyed chanting hall a certain vitality and dignity.

Within moments of arriving, we find ourselves in the hospitable grasp of the aged couple and monk. I never cease to be amazed at the incredible understanding and strength of character of elderly Tibetans. They form the foundation of Tibetan society. *Ama-la* and *pa-la* possess that kindness, hospitality and empathy which immediately makes one feel at home in their presence. It's a quality that comes from their earthy roots and long years of living, but also from the wisdom gained in following Jambayang's lead which teaches that one kindness begets another.

Flashing toothless grins, and with a gentle persistence, they usher us into a modest room dominated by a colorful altar with images of buddhas, butterlamps, water-offering bowls, a photograph of their personal, guiding lama and several large pictures of the Dalai Lama.

My companion, sensing the old folks' deep devotion, presents to them a photograph of the Dalai Lama for their altar. It is probably the most valuable gift that a Tibetan in Tibet (or, for that matter, anywhere) can receive. All day long, each day, everywhere one goes in Tibet, one is constantly asked: *"kuts, kuts, Dalai Lama'i par?"* or *"Yeshe Norbu guba?"*; "please, please, a Dalai Lama photo?", "the Precious Jewel's body being?" Sometimes the "please" can be lost in their dogged persistence, however, and the visitor may tend to become a bit hardened to an otherwise perfectly reasonable request. But generally, one gladly gives this most special of presents, as long as the supply lasts.

To see this gentle old woman touch the photograph to the crown of her head, tears rolling down her cheeks, is—to say the least—a humbling experience which makes one appreciate even life's smallest joys.

Similarly, to speak with the old man, over several cups of tea, concerning the plight of Tibetans makes one exceedingly aware of the preciousness of living.

They clearly have their priorities well ordered. For to experience their devotion to continuing the spiritual work of their culture is to know, on an immediate and practical level, a core element in the wisdom teachings of Jambayang: that knowledge is only as good as the way in which it is applied.

Would but we all dwell on such sacred heights.

The Battle for Iron Mountain

There's a fierce battle raging for the body and spirit of Iron Mountain and, in the process, for the minds of the people on the Altar of the Earth.

The battle can be clearly seen from this vantage point near the peak of Iron Mountain.

But I get ahead of myself; let me backtrack a bit.

Several centuries ago a building was erected at Iron Mountain's summit. It was designed in the venerable Tibetan style and dedicated to healing body, mind and spirit.

The Mendzikhang, Tibetan Medical Institute, thus found a home on the highest free-standing hill in the Lhasa Valley, a sacred peak doubtlessly revered since pre-Buddhist times.

After the advent of Buddhism, Chakpori came to be known to embody some of the life force and clarified mental energy of the fierce-looking bodhisattva of enlightened skilled ways and means, Chana Dorje (Vajrapani in Sanskrit).

Because of the presence of the Medical Institute and the energy of Chana Dorje, people would come to Iron Mountain to show their respect through offerings at the Institute's shrines, and by stringing up countless scores of prayer flags at its summit.

Over the centuries, generations took breath and eventually fell to dust while Iron Mountain remained firmly fixed to the earth with its pinnacle grazing the sky. The prayer flags, strung on lines and impaled at the ends of bundles of tree branches at its summit, unceasingly sent out requests and thanks to Chana Dorje and the other enlightened beings on whom the people relied for aid, and whose qualities they strove toward in their own thoughts and deeds.

In a real sense, the prayer flags were rainbow antennae for sending out signals of supreme spiritual significance. All the more so, considering the unobstructed height from which they flew, here above the valley known as the Place of the Gods.

But the complacency of the Tibetans and the very complexion of Iron Mountain were destined to change dramatically. It's all history, of course: the Chinese takeover and subsequent destruction of holy places—the Medical Institute being one of the most visible victims.

This was, however, hardly the end of the story. The battle for Iron Mountain was yet to begin.

In 1982 the authorities erected, on the site of the former Medical Institute, a massive telecommunications tower for sending television signals out over Central Tibet.

At best, it serves to disseminate numbing entertainment. At worst, its one-sided flow of information is an agent for shoring up a colonial rule in its attempt to convert the Tibetan populace to the wounded ideal of the Marxist/Confucian everyman.

Still, despite the iron fence-enclosed antenna and its circular sentry building, Tibetans continue to climb up here to string their prayer flags to Chana Dorje and the Buddhas. Doubtlessly, in their minds they hope that Iron Mountain's indwelling protector divinity will gather together his skilled energies to throw off this technological profanity.

So, the battle rages, though a subtle one, over Iron Mountain's fate. On one side, the forces of light and goodness. Their foot soldiers are the Buddhist pilgrims and their cavalry, the flapping, rainbow-colored array of "windhorses," the common name for prayer flags.

On the other side of the fence, in the battle for Iron Mountain, are the dark forces of ignorance. Not knowing the ramifications of their own power, or the path of harmony and ease for attaining their elusive goals, they know only how to impose their will upon others who are less materially strong. Theirs is a tough veil of unknowing, of ignoring reality, one which the major nations of the world all, sadly, seem to share.

Their solution to the search for happiness is a great iron fence with electromagnetic garbage spewing forth from a great ugly iron tower, built upon the bones of a place of enlightenment and healing.

Such are the forces assembled at the battleground atop Iron Mountain. The battle's raging here and now, and it's anybody's guess who will win it.

*Whey of the White Clouds**

The high altitude valley, destined in a later era to be called the Place of the Gods, sat unconcerned for centuries over a troubled world more than three thousand meters below its river-scoured plain.

Despite its rugged isolation, among mountains that would dwarf all but the highest in Europe and the Americas, the Lhasa Valley is today being overrun, although in a gentle way. It's yielding to a quiet invasion of the Whey of the White Clouds.

Mountainscapes are among the most enigmatic features on Mother Earth's anatomy. Due to their sheer presence within the depths of the sky, mountains exert a decided influence upon our ocean of air and, in turn, are subjected to the full brunt of its forces.

What, for lowlanders, might be a monolithic and monocromatic gray sky, is for dwellers atop the Altar of the Earth a vivid procession of vapors, caressing and foaming in and around the rocky peaks, like milk's whey about its curds.

The Whey of the White Clouds has witnessed extraordinary changes in the Lhasa Valley, over the centuries.

Perhaps it remembers when the valley was quiet. When the first villages were built from packed earth and stone, by an equally earthy people who produced all that was necessary for living, from their herds and fields.

The whey vapors no doubt remember the three hills that have always stood prominently within the otherwise flat valley cut by the Kyichu River, the Waters of Happiness. Doubtlessly, too, they remember that in the centuries before the advent of Buddhism, these hills were the dwelling places of major divinities of the earth, ones who embodied the very character and energy of the land.

As the centuries passed, the white clouds experienced even more astounding changes in their valley. At first, the changes came like the clouds, slowly and quietly. But as the land yielded its sustenance the people thrived. More and more humans were generated out of the partnership of the fruits of the land and the womenfolk's wombs.

Eventually many more began to arrive at the Place of the Gods from distant valleys, ridges and plains. They streamed in at about the same time that houses of a different kind began to appear among the dwellings of the valley people.

The Tibetans called these *lhakhang*, God's Houses. They were dedicated to new sorts of divinities, embodiments of the powerful landscape of the mind. Their teachings would come to be known by the world below the valley as Buddhism, while the people in the valley would simply call it *Chö*, The Religion.

Built and supported by the people of Lhasa, the *lhakhangs* became associated with *gompas*, solitary communities of individuals dedicated to preserving, teaching and taking on the qualities of their newer gods' thoughts, expressions and actions. Strange to say, these gods were considered as having no actual "self-existence" but were, in the end, emblems of those very same processes and potentials in the mentality of all beings.

Soon, even the three sacred hills had become transformed by the people and their new way of life. The Whey of the White Clouds now swirled over hills dedicated to bodhisattvas, divine embodiments of three active qualities which, when fully developed and held in balance with one another, compose the enlightened, Buddha Mind.

The insinuating mists would swirl about these mountains—Ponpori, Chakpori, and massive Marpori, now dedicated to the divinity who is the unequivocable source of boundless love and compassion issuing from the heart of a buddha. Marpori had become the home of Chenrezi (Avalokiteshvara).

The people had built a great palace at its summit and call it the Potala. Over the centuries it grew organically from out of the massive hilltop. Like Marpori, the Potala juts upward in a graceful gliding motion. It is trapezoidal by necessity, an extension of the very rhythm of the sacred hill.

Within the rock, wood, gold and silken Potala lived the physical embodiments of the mindstream that is Chenrezi. Religious teachers call them *tulkus,* "emanation bodies" of the divinity. Ordinarily, people call them Gwalya Rinpoche or Dalai Lama. Tibetans considered themselves the most fortunate people in the world to have these embodiments of the enlightened mind as spiritual guides, and so close at hand.

With the completion of the Potala and, earlier, the Jokhang cathedral below it, Lhasa had indeed become the Place of the Gods. It was a combined spiritual, residential and commercial center very much like those cities of ancient Egypt and Mexico to which Tibet is sometimes likened.

Lhasa and its people would, in fact, be the last in a long line of unbroken indigenous civilizations that were based upon the laws of the earth and of the spirit, rather than on technology and conquest. Their technical ingenuity was directed toward building huge metaphysical edifices in order to link the earth and sky, those grand spiritual metaphors in whose unity is expressed the oneness of body and mind sought by all.

Up here, in the lower reaches of the stratosphere, the Whey of the White Clouds has borne witness to the growth of a glorious experiment in living. May its eternal passage over the Altar of the Earth bear further witness to its endurance in the centuries to come.

* This essay is dedicated to the memory of Lama Anagarika Govinda. May he quickly return.

THROUGH THE HEARTLAND
GYANGTSE, SHIGATSE AND SAKYA

"I honor the Buddhist faith
which extends like the magnificent waters of Yamdrok Lake."
—*from a contemporary Tibetan folksong*

Place and People

The Lake of Clear Light

One can see every submerged stone, far into the turquoise colored water beyond the shoreline of the Lake of Clear Light.

At an altitude of fourteen thousand seven hundred feet, the placid waters of Lake Yamdrok Tso compose one of the world's highest major inland bodies of water.

Its scorpion-shaped shoreline meanders through a valley surrounded by huge peaks and dotted with innumerable rugged villages built out of the native rock.

Not only is a scorpion a reasonably appropriate description of its physical shape, it's valid in a metaphysical sense, as well.

Scorpions, along with frogs and snakes, are considered terrestrial manifestations of the sentience investing the earth's watery realms: its springs, lakes and rivers. The beings embodying the mind energy of these places are called *lü* or, in Sanskrit, *naga*.

To Tibetans—living as they do in a sundrenched, arid environment—water is crucial to life, health and happiness. And, by its absence, it brings death, illness and misfortune. Accordingly, the *lü* must be periodically recognized and propitiated.

Just the other day, as an example, friends in Lhasa had called the monks into their home to do a ceremony invoking the *lü* for just this very reason. Such a necessary ounce of prevention brings with it the bounty of the *lü* and forestalls the need for a future cure.

The *lü* are visualized in their most sublime forms as male and female figures that are human from the waist up but serpentine from below. Imagine a mermaster and mermaid with lower torsos in the form of snakes.

In palaces, at the bottom of their waters, they have amassed untold riches—sunken treasures in the form of *norbu*, brightly shining wish-fulfilling jewels. Exist in peace and harmony with the *lü* energy, and your life will progress as if it were full of wish-fulfilling jewels.

Yamdrok Tso is itself like a glowing jewel when viewed from the tundra-covered heights overlooking it. In the intense sunlight it glints alternately turquoise green then lapis blue, sending off variegated reflections of sunlight and cloud-dotted sky that surely can be seen from orbit.

Its purest reflections can be seen from an even more rarified vantage point. It seems to the inner eye, at this moment, to be radiating invisible rays of light of the same order as that which permeates our internal depths, our personal waters of consciousness. One knows that this intensely reflective lake gives off a kind of clear light similar to the refined clear light of consciousness which is at the basis of every sentient being's mental processes. This mind light is, in turn, the same stuff composing the Great Void, which is the undifferentiated source of all phenomena.

Rather than being solid, corporeal, "real," Yamdrok Tso is actually ever changing. Its momentary characteristics are determined by the observer's physical perspective and the point in time at which it is viewed.

All human beings, due to generally similar experiences, mutually agree that this is a lake. They assume that since it possesses all the required physical attributes, it has a quality of self-existence, much as one thinks of oneself as existing. Meditators who have lived for long periods of time above its shores, see it another way: as a glowing figment of the imagination, as a phantom no more real than a mirage. They have found that its existence is ultimately an interplay of the powers of the imagination and the infinitely varying reflections bouncing about in this magical spot on the Altar of the Earth.

No longer a particular lake, it is of the essence of clear light, a phenomenom embodied equally in lakes and mountains, humans and earthworms.

Doubtlessly, countless meditators, lamas, fortunate travelers and villagers living along its shores have sensed the lake's grand metaphor, its inner qualities. In so doing, they've gained a bit of the psychic wealth of the wish-fulfilling jewels glowing below the shiny waters of the Lake of Clear Light.

The Spirit of Tibet

The elderly monks are in a most cordial and humor-filled state of mind as they motion this foreign traveler into the dark recesses of their old monastery's chanting hall.

We shuffle past huge statues of the protectors of the four quarters of our universe. Then, along a wall mural of the *Sipai Korlo*, the Wheel of the Transmigration of the Consciousness, which reminds us of the constant rounds of rebirth taken by our mental shades. It shows the realms of rebirth possible in *samsara*, this world of illusion and suffering into which we are born, the reasons for being on its unmerry-go-round, and the means for jumping free of it.

On the other side of the entranceway, so vividly painted as to be almost floating away from its wall, a second mural further describes the mental posture needed to jump the wheel. It shows a flaming sword, that of the bodhisattva Jambayang (Manjushri). The sword signifies his qualities of transcendental wisdom which, when wielded properly, can cut through the veil of ignorance clouding one's potentially enlightened nature.

Then, suddenly, we find ourselves in the cool, dark, butter aroma-saturated precincts of the chanting hall of Gyangtse's

Paljor Chöde Monastery.

We pass an elderly couple engaged in strenuous, full prostrations at the rear of the hall while a group of homespun wool-clad laymen and two young monks sit off in one corner.

We walk to the front of the hall and find the shrine bearing the statue of Sakyamuni Buddha in his refined form, known as the Jo Rinpoche. It's an essential image to have in any monastery's temple, but particularly one such as Paljor Chöde. It has become a sacred space ecumenical to all four Tibetan sects, in compensation for the lack of available facilities since the widespread destruction during the cultural revolution. In lieu of statues specific to a single sect, the Jo serves to symbolize the ultimate perfection of mind, a goal shared by all *Vajrayana*, Tantric Buddhists.

"*Gusho-la, ya pey, deyshu,*" comes the kindly but forceful invitation from the seated group at the corner of the hall: "Respected sir, do come in, sit down;" this invitation has always been, in past interactions, a sure indicator of a most pleasant way of getting in touch with new people, events and places on the Altar of the Earth.

I am hardly seated on the monks' cushions when my hand is firmly captured by an elderly man, "dressed to the nines" in a black, homespun Tibetan jacket and matching pants, set off by a multicolored sash and boots, also of native wool.

Soon come the burning questions: "Where are you from?" "How did you learn Tibetan?" "Who is your teacher?" "What do you do?" and so on. I answer them as best I can, in the course of which sensing that my Tibetan is not only returning to its previous state of non-fluency but is actually gaining new ground remarkably quickly. Baptisms in fire such as this are the only way of learning a language, and of internalizing a way of life and thought different from one's own.

Then comes the obligatory English lesson, at their request: "*Tashi deley, kaley pey* and *kaley shu* is hello, goodbye."

"How do you say *djokpo pepsho* in English?"

"Come back soon," I reply.

And so it goes.

Then come the frequently heard observations about the current state of affairs in Tibet and their hopes for the future. Always the same lament; it breaks my heart to hear it from such sincere and suffering people.

The conversation and English lesson complete, I join up with an old man who guides me around the monastery's grounds. We go around in a clockwise, sunwise fashion, as is the custom of Tibetan Buddhists, indeed all natural and nature-aware peoples the world around.

The focal points of our circumambulation include the temple, its attendant shrine buildings and, particularly, the great chörten, built five centuries ago. One need only take a seat along this well-worn path to eventually see all of Tibet walk by, as the chörten is a major stop on every pilgrimage to Central Tibet.

Hand in hand, we walk along. An instantaneous bond arises between us. It transcends culture, language and roots separated by half a world.

It's a special experience, let me tell you, to walk this way with a man having a history so different from one's own, around a place that has been sanctified by centuries of people, doing daily what we are doing now.

After several circumambulations we prepare to say goodbye, with the plan of meeting the next morning for more conversation.

I take my leave, saying that I must do one more *korwa*, another circumambulation. I feel the need to do it for its spiritual value as well as to take advantage of the lovely sun-setting light for some photography.

But before the camera can come out I am captured by another wonderful homespun gentleman and his charming Tibetan wife, for another round of circumambulations.

They volunteer the altogether too commonly heard story of Tibet; how they have suffered and how much the Dalai Lama means to them. They convey it seriously, like the monks who guided me within the monastery's temple, but with a light-heartedness—tinged with a certain sadness—and a conspicuous absence of anger.

I truly appreciate the forthright and friendly conversation that one constantly finds among these materially simple but spiritually sophisticated people.

For they are the spirit of Tibet.

A Taste of the Earth

"We've got many ways of preparing *dru*, each for a different purpose. You're now having it two ways. The barley's flour is roasted into *tsampa* and fermented into *chang*. We call the mixture you're eating *pak*," explains Ringzin.

I'd eaten *pak* on many occasions while living with Tibetans in India. They had prepared the *tsampa* and *chang* themselves but had to import the barley kernels from fields that were many thousands of feet higher than their Himalayan foothill settlements. Today, however, I'm experiencing the entire process of barley culture in a most alimentary manner.

Imagine the setting. After leaving the rocky pathways of Tsechen Village, I set my sights on the town of Gyangtse, hovering in the distance at the end of a mud and gravel road paralleling the turbulent Nyangchu River.

Turning back, one last view of the village reveals a pastoral place: old-style stone houses, prayer flags, sweet snotty-faced children and inquisitive adults. I ponder my meetings with the villagers; how I'd spent hours trying to answer their questions about myself and my life in a world that, to them, must certainly have sounded like it was Mars. I also tried to inform them, as best I could, of how my world was beginning to impinge on their doorsteps. It seemed the only right thing to do.

With such memories and impressions still fresh in mind, I begin to walk around Tsechen Mountain in order to get a closer look at ruins on a small hillock there. Just then, from out of the corner of my eye, I spy a low adobe building and people waving vigorously at me.

Naturally, I walk over and greet them with a *tashi deley!*

"*Tashi deley*, come here, sit down," the old man Ringzin and his wife Pasang welcome me. They are sitting with several young women—one with an infant in tow—on a pile of rocks and earth, eating *pak*.

"Have some of this *tsampa* and *chang*," says Ringzin as he offers me my first *pak* in Tibet. All around us, amid irrigation ditches leading from the Nyangchu River, grows the barley from which came the *tsampa* and *chang* we are now eating. Casting my gaze around me I notice a captured reservoir of river water spilling into two ditches which disappear under the building. Then the mind becomes aware of a whirring, grinding sound.

A mill?

"We call it *chota*," Ringzin explains. It is, in fact, a fairly large mill whose water-run grinding stones no doubt supply much of Tsechen Village's barley meal needs.

How long have Tibetans like Ringzin and Pasang been grinding their barley in this manner? Surely it dates back tens of centuries, to the dim past during which the Neolithic Revolution found its way up to the hunters and gatherers ranging over the Altar of the Earth.

Their millstones are the kinds of wheels of which we need more in this world. This is appropriate technology, one that sustains life, unlike their cousins belonging to automobiles and tanks, which turn life into a careening and sometimes deadly rollercoaster ride.

And even more than millstones, what our "modern" society and its messiahs of progress particularly need, is that tasty wisdom that I'm internalizing today. A lesson that can only be learned, it seems, by traveling to distant places such as Tibet.

It is a lesson of "wholing," of being at one with the entire process of living, of being aware of every turning of the great wheel of life.

Like Ringzin, Pasang and the others of Tsechen Village, we too must learn to plant, cultivate and then to thankfully harvest with our thoughts, verbalizations and deeds. And it must all be done with a good heart. Only then can we fully enjoy the fruits of our harvest.

We must become "in tune"; take responsibility for the totality of things in our psychic, social and physical environments. We must, in short, become universal men and women.

This is hardly a luxury from a bygone age. It's a necessity of this age and of those to come.

In the course of bidding goodbye to Ringzin, Pasang and their family, we mutually observe that despite obvious differences in our appearances, languages and mannerisms, we are, down deep, all the same: "*semlo chikpa re*," "in consciousness, we are one."

At that moment my mind—like their food with their crops—is at one with their own. We are of one mind in our unspoken wish that such oneness might be so for all people, in all places, and in all times to come.

The River and I

It's an old song, this love affair between a man and a river.

It's always been my song, one quite preferable to those sung about the oceans. For in its setting, a river can seem equally as powerful as the great font of life into which it flows.

The thoughts come flowing beside this roaring artery called the Nyangchu River, as it pumps the life's blood of Tibet into the great aorta of the Yarlung Tsangpo River.

If the lush, green fields of barley and wheat alongside it are any indication, then the people of Gyangtse too must hold it in awe. For their very lives depend upon the Nyangchu's surging waters.

Rivers such as this are much more than means of mass irrigation in high altitude valleys. They are the elixir of life, a fertile decoction of all the minerals composing the incredible Plateau of Tibet.

In the West, similar brews are now bought in stores. But unwholesome and unnatural chemical fertilizers cannot begin to do what this mountain's soup does for Tibet's people and land. "You are what you eat" takes on particular significance beside this boiling river.

The Nyangchu can be so powerful—as during this present

snow melt season—that its benevolence has sometimes turned into tragedy. Not many years ago, in fact, Gyangtse's fertile and well-watered soil was inundated by a massive flood. Even today, one sees the people digging ditches in and around the town to ease the pressure of excess water.

Excess water in arid Tibet? Such is the personality of a great river fed by melting glaciers.

Sitting here, along its hand-hewn, masonry-reinforced banks, one gets a very different view of Gyangtse's towering fortress, monastery and *chörten* than from in town. One sees a massive mountain looming behind it, like the perfect backdrop to an infinitesimally slow dance. One can take in the superb symmetry of the scene with a sweeping glance. It all shows the natural collaboration of earth and water, the two principles of life— male and female—in an eternal *pas de deux*.

But a full three hundred and sixty degree view is necessary to fully appreciate the perfection of the place: a limitless sky, broken only by high mountains looking like hills; and a valley of green fields and rocky villages, cut by a river forever flowing.

It all seems perfectly right.

Like the river, like its old familiar tune, thoughts and feelings come easily flowing on the Altar of the Earth.

Invasion of the Booty Snatchers

The stone parapet, here, atop the great *dzong* of Gyangtse, Fortress of the Peak of Kings, silently stretches into the sky. It provides a commanding view, in all directions, of the spreading Nyangchu River Valley.

Since earliest times, Gyangtse and its valley have been one of Tibet's major agricultural "breadbaskets" and the most important center for trade of wool between Tibet and its lowland neighbors to the south.

Gyangtse has also been a significant center of religious commerce. Successive generations had dedicated an entire mountainside to a complex of monastic halls, shrines and associated facilties. And in their midst had risen, during the fifteenth century, one of the most significant Buddhist monuments on the Altar of the Earth, known as the Kumbum *chörten*, the *chörten* of One Hundred Thousand Buddha Images.

From this place, atop the *dzong's* immense stone battlements, the Kumbum *chörten's* golden crown glints hotly in the intense sunlight. The *chörten* stands relatively alone against the bare mountainside, save for the temple of Paljor Chöde Monastery and the few associated buildings that have survived since earlier times. During the past century Gyangtse has fallen upon hard times, enduring successive invasions of booty snatchers.

The invasions began around the year 1904. Then, as the third most important city in Tibet, it bustled with nomads who would come down from the high grasslands with huge herds of sheep and yak, while traders from Nepal, Sikkim and Bhutan would bring their wares and lowland foodstuffs up to the high valley in order to acquire the nomads'dried meat, wool and salt gathered from the great lakes dotting their steppe lands. Money? What was that? Barter was the name of the game.

Given its disparate visitors and activities, Gyangtse must have been a vibrant community, with a rich quality of life that comes from people living in a natural sort of way.

I base these assumptions upon life in Gyangtse today, as well as yesterday. It is, despite the severe problems faced throughout Tibet, an exceedingly hospitable and friendly place. In Gyangtse people literally come out and greet you from their adobe and stone houses, houses that are gaily bedecked with prayer flags and auspicious symbols such as swastikas, sun and moon, and wish-fulfilling jewels.

Given Gyangtse's excellent setting, in a broad waterfed valley with more than enough crops for the people's needs, it is quite evident to the mind's eye that this was, in 1904, a most fortunate place in which to live.

But the good fortune was shattered with the coming of British troops, under the direction of a young diplomat named Younghusband and a hard-boiled general. They presented the Tibetan authorities in Gyangtse with a clear-cut ultimatum: open up trade with us, or else.

Living in blissful semi-isolation atop the roof of the world, and priding themselves on being fine warriors—in the conventional hand to hand manner—the Tibetans understandably resisted what to them seemed a barbaric overture. But the British expedition's artillery power and crack Gurkha infantry far outmatched the Tibetans and their archaic equipment within the *dzong*. It eventually fell, at the cost of many hundreds of Tibetan lives. It is said that the grim reality of this carnage had a great effect upon Younghusband and that after his arrival in Lhasa, he had a profound personal awakening which resulted in his dedicating the rest of his life to humanitarian pursuits. One suspects that the rude awakening of the Gyangtse experience plus the natural power of Tibet's land, in concert with the intense spirituality of its people, all worked toward this end.

A changed Younghusband notwithstanding, the British finally withdrew, secure in the knowledge that a tiny bit, at least, of the booty of this fabled land would consistently come their way. To their credit, the British knew when it was time to leave—to leave Tibet's sovereignty to the Tibetans. But in doing a right thing, perhaps they inadvertently did a wrong. Tibetan sovereignty would not last very long. Fifty years of tranquility would be rudely shattered by the invasion of another horde of booty snatchers whose belief in a manifest destiny of controlling Tibet resulted in a major cultural holocaust.

Ask any Chinese person from Taipei, Hong Kong or Beijing for his opinion on the Tibetan Question. The answer will generally run something like this: "Why Tibet has always been a part of China." That a predominantly single ethnicity, the Han Chinese, can assume this, despite overwhelming cultural evidence to the contrary, is very much like the views of nineteenth-century White Americans concerning the Indians and their lands.

"Go west, young man," Horatio Alger's horrifying colonial exhortation, is as applicable to the Chinese annexation of Tibet as its was to America a hundred years ago: "Go west young man. The land is free for the taking; it's empty land (never mind the Indians, they're barbarians after all)." And so it goes. The rest is history.

The rest is history in Tibet, as well, although the events are fresher and the wounds still fester. After the desecrations and killings culminating in the cultural revolution, Tibet was left to lick its wounds. It's spiritual life's blood was essentially all that it had left to sustain itself. Grain, butter and meat were rationed. The grim specter of "equality," engendered through mass starvation, became known for the first time. In addition to the many tens of thousands of People's Liberation Army mouths that required feeding, a disastrous agricultural policy demanding the cultivation of wheat rather than the indigenous, high altitude-adapted barley, added another dimension to the suffering imposed on these gentle people of the Altar of the Earth.

Enter the 1980's, and the Chinese government's swing toward social and economic pragmatism. In this highly structured society, still seeming to be more Confucian than communist, the bulk of the population has directed its thoughts and energies toward a new policy of acquisition of booty. The catch phrase that one consistently hears nowadays in China, and in its borderland territories, is "economic modernization" through the acquisition of foreign countries' technological know-how and their "hard" currencies.

Consider, for a moment, the severe social and psychological problems brought about—in Western countries—by this form of "economic modernization." They are the very same ones that you and I have contended with all our lives and have "worked out" with varying degrees of success. And I'm sure you'll wonder, as do I, about the ultimate results of this approach to happiness in today's China.

I'm particularly led to wonder about the effects of modernization here in Gyangtse, when I meet its friendly people on their rounds of the monastery and *chörten* and as they market and socialize on its streets. I'm afraid for them, in the same way that I've become afeared that Lhasa, the fabled capital, is already well on its way to a severe case of modernitis. One Lhasaite recently remarked, "We've got English fever." Translated loosely this means: "We all want to learn English so that we can communicate more effectively with tourists and partake of their 'neat' materialism." All well and good, if things are kept in perspective and balance. Time will tell if this is the case.

It's interesting, isn't it, how opposites seem always to attract in this world of *samsara*. We come to Tibet to seek out a way of life and thought that may inspire us to balance our-

selves within the shallow morass of Western civilization, while
some Tibetans latch on to our materialism, trusting that it will
help better their lives; make them free. What we don't seem
to realize is that we are all players upon the stage of a black
comedy. And darkening the plot is the fact that, while the
comedy is directed by the parties presently in control of Tibet,
they themselves are equally unaware of the toll exacted by their
desired materialism, that which already controls every aspect
of life in the West.

I'm starting to see it all quite clearly now, from this tower
atop the citadel of Gyangtse. Just below, the most recent edifice
of the latest booty snatchers in Tibet is under construction.
A huge and architecturally inappropriate tourist hotel is being feverishly constructed by non-Tibetan labor. Ironically, the
sponsors of this hotel are at a loss as to why anyone would
be interested in visiting these Tibetan "barbarians." Still, as
long as the tourists desire to come, they will be obliged...for
a stiff fee, of course. No bargaining or bartering permitted.

Huge tourist hotels are being built all over Tibet at a
breakneck pace, in order to service well meaning, but themselves intrusive, foreign tourists. Once this "luxury class" hotel
is completed it seems inevitable that its cost will not only be
high to the travelers but also to the Tibetans of Gyangtse, who
will see little of the profits realized from the tourists.

Experience in other parts of Tibet teaches that a suddenly
active tourist environment changes the rules of the game of
life for the local people. They are placed under much greater
stress than before. Certainly some incidental wealth comes their
way. But for the most part, they lose. They can no longer participate in everyday life with the same nonchalance and
anonymity.

Looking down toward the *chörten* and monastery complex,
I can just make out life on a tiny street parallel to the larger,
main street of Gyangtse. It's one that is normally invisible to
casual tourists. Its a street of family homes; of cows milling
freely with smiling, dirty faced children. A street of teenage
boys and girls meeting intensely with their eyes. A place for

easy, early evening conversations and strolls in the cool night air.

What will become of these people? How will their lives be improved by tourist currency flowing to Beijing? How will they become enriched by a telephoto lens being practically rammed down their unconsenting throats by an unthinking tourist? How will their lives be benefited by hordes of unreflective and acquisitive visitors bulldozing their frantic ways down a once quiet lane, a tiny communal refuge from decades of suffering and booty snatching?

How indeed? For in essence, my friends, far from being part of the solution we are now part of the problem. We, like the government that currently exerts its influence over the Altar of the Earth, and the British before them, are also booty snatchers. Snatchers of the booty of Tibetan exotica.

Still, we have an opportunity to do some good when we come to Tibet. We can give back to these kind and open-hearted people an even more valuable prize. We can show respect and a modicum of human concern. We can be mindful of our dress and act respectfully in their communities and places of holiness. We can ask permission to take a photograph. Sign language works perfectly fine for the purpose. And, take my advice, when the person collaborates with you the result is far superior than the "snap and run" kind.

We can indeed talk to the people through gestures, after all isn't a picture worth a thousand words? We can begin to establish person to person links and in the process gain a deeper understanding of the thoughts, feelings and ways of life of the Children of the Snows.

If enough of us walk the streets of the Gyangtses of Tibet with an awakened attitude,the Tibetans' lives will become less drastically altered, while ours will become enriched without it happening at their expense.

Two booty snatchers in one century are quite enough; let's jump off that grotesque carousel.

Enough said.

Welcome to the Altar of the Earth.

Spirit

One Hundred Thousand Paths to a Buddha

Multiplicity and height are useful to Tibetans as metaphors for launching into the stratosphere of enlightenment.

Multiply your prayers and contemplations by devices such as invocation-bearing prayer flags and prayer wheels.

Reflect upon innumerable images of deities, those enlightened beings manifesting a particular quality of a buddha's thoughts, expressions and actions.

Always look toward physical heights: mountain peaks or towering monuments such as *chörtens*. Let the power of your imaginations transform the peak or *chörten* into the Axis of the Universe, the pedestal of a glorious temple of a buddha. The temple's halls—made from rainbow-colored light—float upon lotus-shaped clouds that crown the apex of the cosmic peak called Mount Meru.

Through the power of your imagination, try to become those many buddhas manifesting the infinite qualities of the enlightened mind in their palatial temples at the top of the universe.

Having internalized this set of mind you can, I think, fully appreciate the great edifice rising before me.

From the old stone steps of Paljor Chöde *gompa's* temple the view is dominated by the Kumbum (One Hundred Thousand Bodies—Images—of a Buddha) *chörten* (Basis of the *Dharma* Teachings).

Much has been said about the psychospiritual meaning of the *chörten*. One learns that its architectural features signify the five alchemical elements: the square base being earth; the circular girdle, water; the conical spire, fire; the dish-like feature atop the spire, air; and the flame-like jewel, capping it all, space or mind.

One also learns that these five features are related to five colors—yellow, blue, red, green and white, colors one also sees in rainbows of innumerable prayer flags fluttering in high places.

On a more subtle level, one comes to learn that each color and element refers to a different "family" of tantric buddhas. They all coexist in an harmoniously structured universe called a *mandala*. This *mandala* is, at once, the infinite universe and a universal temple or palace that is situated atop Mount Meru. Each is related to a different aspect of one's psychophysical being (one's form and mental functions) and, in turn, holds the key to certain wisdoms that lead the way to enlightenment.

These five tantric buddhas are thus emblems and guides to an integrated way of thinking, expressing and doing. They are envisioned to emanate—to differentiate—into various *yidams*, divine teachers who show specific enlightened characteristics and the means of attaining them.

These five buddha families, in turn, are emanations themselves of an even more sublime reality, one embodied in the Primordial, Adi Buddha, the undifferentiated, enlightened mind that is at one with the cosmos.

Not surprisingly, one learns that the *chörten* is considered the quintessential physical expression of the mind of a buddha and, by extension, the Primordial Buddha's consciousness.

With these thoughts in mind, I stand here, at Gyangtse's most sacred Buddhist shrine, poised to enter the largest *chörten* remaining in Tibet. I am about to surround myself with phys-

ical expressions of the Adi Buddha's mental energy; to explore
a multiplicity of artistic expressions of the enlightened mind
and to consider their meaning to the progress of my own developing consciousness.

I climb up the *chörten's* many dark, steep stairwells to explore this ultimate "outer" expression of the Adi Buddha's
mandala. And if I can keep my mind's eyes sufficiently open,
I may find the means of revealing the Primordial Buddha's
light within the *mandala* of my own reality.

It's very much like a quest as I strive upward and inward
into the *mandala.* It begins on the ground level (its edge, when
viewed from above as one does in the usual two-dimensional
representations of *mandalas*).

Four powerful protectors stand guard at the narrow entry-
way into this hub of the Buddha Mind. In their "outer" forms
as large statues, they insure that no harm comes to the sacred
images, which have resided within since the fifteenth century. Their "inner," subtle forms have, similarly, protected all
sentient beings living on continents, floating to the four directions in a primeval sea, around the slopes of Mount Meru.

Upward and inward one strives. Up through a vestibule
painted with images of goddesses insuring long life for all. Then
comes a hallway, populated by fierce protector divinities. They
stand sentry to dispel not only external obstacles but also the
negativity arising from tainted thoughts which otherwise might
pollute this pure buddha realm.

They are there to dispel the five major kinds of mental obscurations or neuroses, which afflict us all to varying degrees,
and which can be fully cured only through the antidote of the
enlightened wisdom of the five buddha families.

So these fierce emanations of the Primordial Buddha are the
very energies which we must summon from within in order
to aid our progress toward enlightenment.

Continuing upward into the precincts of the Buddha Mind,
one enters a level populated by statues of four buddhas, each
facing into a cardinal direction. Their gazes take in the enor-
mity of the Gyangtse-Nyangchu Valley through four elaborately

decorated portals. Their directional orientation reinforces the inner message of the *mandala*, suggesting the solid foundation of two crossed lines meeting at a center, this center being the Primordial Buddha consciousness.

Although I am amid buddhas (in their outer forms at least), I'm hardly home free. For in one's upward pilgrimage toward more subtle realms of mind one must constantly be reminded of the intense energy needed to dispel primordial ignorance. So now comes another gallery of fierce divinities, at the head of a narrow, steep stairway.

These distinctive divinities are actually two in one; male and female in sexual union. Such beings are of the tantric tutelary tradition. They signify the powerful connection that must be established between the male energy of methodical compassion and that wisdom of enlightenment which is the female energy of the divine consciousness.

Another set of stairs brings the pilgrim to a stage below the highest level in his quest for "at-one-ness" with the Adi Buddha. Here, on the four sides of a square masonry pillar, are painted the representations of four of the most essential tantric deities. These *yabyum yidam*, "Father-Mother" tutelaries, are emblems of long and demanding programs of mental and physical yogas that when assiduously practiced—the lamas tell us—can lead to the realization of enlightenment in a single lifetime.

Offhand, I can readily recognize two *yidams*. Here is Tunkhor, Kalachakra, Lord of the Cycles Beyond Time and emblem of the most complex tantra of *Vajrayana* Buddhism. And there, around the corner, the fundamental *yidam*, Demchok or Samvara as he/she is known in Sanskrit. Demchok is the major divinity of Kang Rinpoche, Mount Kailas. The holiest mountain on the Tibetan Plateau, it is considered the natural embodiment of Mount Meru itself.

Other figures of *yidams* materialize then, and as quickly, fade back into the poorly illuminated recesses of the *chörten*. There, partially hidden by the stairs, is Naro Khadroma or Vajra Yogini, the "Sky Dancing Dakini of the Sage Naropa," the "*Yogini* of the Diamond Scepter." She is one of the greatest *yidams*, a magnetizer of egos. She attracts, by seemingly lascivious means, the lustful urges generated by one's uncontrolled ego, then destroys them with her fierce energy. Her tantra is said to be most useful for Westerners.

With Vajra Yogini fading back into the darkness, I climb up into the uppermost chapel of the Kumbum, arriving within its massive golden, conical area. I am quietly greeted by an elderly monk who prays and sits watch over an altar containing several gold and bejeweled statues of Dorje Chang (Vajradhara) considered to be the Adi Buddha by many practitioners of Tantric Buddhism.

So finally, I stand within the inner sanctum of his universal temple. I have completed my journey to the indivisible source of all mind and reality, from a fragmented world of illusion. I have passed through numerous stations of manifold deities, assumedly heeding their lessons and internalizing their qualities. In the process, seeds have been planted into my mind and I may have come just a bit closer to realizing the mind of enlightenment.

Finally, if the monk is willing, one climbs into the rooftop area of the *chörten*—that feature associated with the alchemical element of air—to look out over the mountain-studded, green valley with newly enlightened eyes.

And if the *chörten* experience has been successful, one has also caught a glimpse of the Primordial Buddha Mind through the partnership of the thousands of images within this mountain-like edifice and the determination of one's own effort.

The God Must Be Pleased

The *zhidag*, Master of the Rocky Ridge, must be pleased.

After many long years of enforced quiescence, the great edifices located on high points on either end of his ridge have, like the modest town below them, come to life in an unequivocable way.

The already intense, morning sun breaks over the *zhidag's* shrine, situated on a hump of shale, midway along the weather-worn ridge called Norburi, Mountain of Wish-Fulfilling Jewels. The site commands an unobstructed view of Paljor Chöde Monastery and its enormous Kumbum *chörten*. These edifices are critical to the continuance of the *Vajrayana* form of Buddhism in this region of Tibet. And the local people know that they remain there at the pleasure of the *zhidag*.

Likewise, they understand the special powers of the ancient earth religion of Tibet embodied in the *zhidag*. For these may well have been responsible for the continuing presence of the great fortress that rises dramatically on the opposite end of the ridge. As the only *dzong* among seventy to have escaped destruction since 1959, it is obvious to the Tibetans that the *zhidag* is a powerful earth protector.

Huddling below the *zhidag's* ridge are the people's homes,

looking like an enormous honeycomb of adobe and rock. From here they appear more like extrusions from the earth than like structures made by the human hand. In their very forms they reveal the tenuousness of life below the *zhidag's* heights, a life nourished by fields of barley and vegetables under the guidance of the *zhidag* and his associate, the *sadag*, Master of the Earth.

Indeed, within every natural feature—from the springs to the highest peaks—there is, it is said, a sentience that holds forth from within.

Since well before the advent of Buddhism, Tibetan thinkers and mystics had delved deeply into the inner identity of the land, in order to decipher its foremost qualities and to come into harmony with them. Accordingly, here at a significant pro-truberance, near the center of the massive ridge about which the community of Gyangtse has sprouted (like the barley fields surrounding it all), the people come to hang their colorful pray-er flags from cords and tree branches. It is a spot which the *zhidag* no doubt finds quite adequate for viewing the magnifi-cent Gyangtse-Nyangchu Valley spreading beyond it.

In addition to invoking the major Buddhist deities to pro-vide health, wealth and liberation from suffering for all sen-tient beings, the flags also call out to the Master of the Rocky Ridge, encouraging the *zhidag* to continue his benevolence toward their lovely valley and its ancient town, in this verdant corner of Tibet.

The god must be pleased.

A Fierce Legacy

It's a fixture in most monasteries and one finds it, indeed, in Gyangtse's Paljor Chode *gompa*. It's a special place, off in the dark recesses of an already darkly-lit building. It's a place of fierce, dark beings who nonetheless are dedicated to that light and goodness at the heart of Tibetan Buddhism. Contradictory though it seems, all becomes clear when one considers how Tibetans view their lives.

Their world—their reality—is one of infinite potential. In it, every being is capable of attaining a paradisic state beyond the psychic and physical suffering with which we are shackled in the course of living.

While they celebrate the beauty and peacefulness of life, Tibetans know full well the horrors and injustices of the world. Living atop the rugged Tibetan Plateau, they are ever aware of the perennial struggle between life and death.

They also know that good thoughts, words and deeds are sometimes not enough, and that a little bit of forceful help is sometimes needed. So, Tibetans sometimes take protective measures to counteract the negative, particularly in the case of their religion which they know must be preserved at all costs.

Enter the protectors of the religion. Their aid is requested here in the murky depths of the *gönkhang*, a room whose name derives from *gonpo*, "protector being" and *khangba*, "house"; literally Protector's House. All beings need a home, after all.

The protectors live—on the subtle plane—in fire-illumined places, inhospitable to human beings. But they also emanate—manifest—into various physical forms readily perceptible and comprehensible to us. Some forms, such as the statues sequestered in the *gönkhang*, were made by human hands, while the powers of the visualizations of lamas and monks have sealed the subtle energies of the fiercest protectors of Buddhism into them through a process called "opening the deity's eyes.

Here is Ekajati, the terrifying-looking mother of the fiercest female protectors. She is often called the Single Plait Goddess as she has but one eye, one fang and one single breast, located centrally in their respective bodily areas.

Next in line, along one wall of the chapel, is a massive statue of the Great Black One, Mahakhala, a major protector of the form of Buddhism practiced in Tibet. Many offerings lay before and on the statue, in the form of butterlamps and *khatag* greeting scarves, to insure his continuing services. He is also invoked for his power in dispelling those self-generated obstacles clouding our minds, which are equally as counterproductive to the work of Buddhism as are ghosts and demons, perhaps more so.

Finally, most deeply into the darkness, one can just make out the fierce Palden Lhamo, protectress of Dalai Lamas and the Tibetan state. She rides a snorting wild ass whose saddle is draped with the likeness of a human skin. Her gaping fangs, dark skin, halo of fire, tiara of skulls and fierce demeanor are marvelous symbols of her unbridled yet eminently welcomed power in the service of goodness.

All three figures are very difficult to see, given the profound darkness broken only by butterlamp light and the veils and scarves draped over the images to increase their mystery and psychological impact.

Surrounding them, on the *gonkhang's* walls, are murals issuing out of the fertile Tibetan imagination. They show a paradise of the protectors, one populated by skeletons, consuming infernos and ghoul-like figures of all gruesome description.

Rather than shrinking from them in digust, one realizes that, except for their dramatic value, they are images of powerful forces within our own psyches which can ultimately work for the good.

Certainly, Tibetans are many steps ahead of our culture's understanding in this regard. We go to horror films for the titillation they bring to our unstable egos. Tibetans, on the other hand, turn dramatic horror into lessons for pursuing the path to enlightenment. Their terrific beings do not reinforce the illusory dichotomy of good and evil—as do the fierce creatures of our literature and films. Theirs are protectors who dispel external obstacles to the religion and internal ones to our enlightenment.

So arise the thoughts, at about the same speed as do the eyes adjust to the low light in this Protector's House. Instead of being put off by the statues, masks, implements and paintings, one gains an unusually secure feeling from the fierce legacy, deep within the minds and monasteries atop the Altar of the Earth.

Time Will Tell

The skeletons stand staunchly in place. Once boldly painted in white, maroon and black, the Gods' Houses, monks' residences, and chanting and assembly halls of the monastery are now gaunt, weathering adobe and stone skeletons amid dangerously loose mounds of rocky scree.

They are remnants of the once thriving body of a communal organism, not unlike a hive of bees. Here, the monastery called Tsechen Chöde, The Great Peak Seat of the Religion, once buzzed with life. Its mountaintop location, above a stone and adobe village of the same name, provided an inspiring view of the Gyangtse-Nyangchu Valley to the three hundred monks who worked, studied and prayed here, in symbiosis with the villagers below them. Together, they propogated a uniquely Tibetan (but at the same time, universal) way of life and spirit in this lovely corner of the Altar of the Earth.

The wide setting, when viewed from amid the ruins: the bustle of activity going on below as the villagers repair their road, clean houses, tend to the animals and unclog irrigation ditches in their fields, make this vertical graveyard ever the more unsettling.

In a real sense, the bones of Tsechen Chöde Monastery,

188 *Altar of the Earth*

flensed of their flesh by the "liberators" in 1962, represent not only the tragedy of old Tibet. They also suggest the challenges of today, and the hopes of Tibetans for the future.

Tsechen Monastery's Tibet was a society that had been basically in harmony within itself and with the inexpressible universe beyond it. During the previous twelve hundred years it had developed a way of living and thinking that satisfied, reasonably well, the people's needs and desires.

This was a period coinciding with the advent of Buddhism: the *Mahayana* strain which was infused with the dynamism of the *Vajrayana*, the tantric method. It was brought from India by inspired teachers who skillfully facilitated its being understood and incorporated into the lives of wild mountain folk of the Tibetan Plateau.

Over the centuries, a distinctly Tibetan form of society and religion took shape, founded upon an awareness of the spirit of place and the liberating theology of Buddhism.

Facilitating the preservation of its religion was the *sangha*: the monks, nuns, teachers, and those guiding lamas who were considered *tulkus*, beings who consciously determined their successive incarnations, in order to work for the welfare of others.

The seeds of the *sangha* were sown from India, but the way they sprouted and flowered was directly the result of the environment in which they were planted and watered.

So, the fact that the monastery and *sangha* became so utterly essential to the Tibetan spiritual way of life is, it appears from this vantage point, the result of the existing Tibetan mental and social environment.

Monasteries great and small were built in breathtaking spots, such as Tsechen Mountain. Along with them sprang up villages. Each worked on behalf of the other. The monasteries needed the villagers' aid in securing food to sustain the monks' bodies; the villagers needed the monks' and lamas' guidance as food for their souls.

That it worked well is clear from the relative success of Tibetan refugee communities in India and Nepal.

But that all was yesterday.

One wonders what will be the ultimate fate of the people inside Tibet, given their limited access to religious and moral guidance. A brief excursion through Tsechen Village suggests that, for the time being, ancient waters and thoughts run deeply. Villagers—those conserving or "traditional" people everywhere— are slow to change their ways. A life close to the earth keeps them wary of new, "quick fixes."

No, it's the people of the cities about whom I worry most. Out there, at the end of the valley, softly floats the "city" of Gyangtse. It is yet a pleasant place, mainly because it has been relatively forgotten by the powers that be. But Gyangtse is beginning to feel the allure of money, foreign values and their material goods. Will Gyangtse's people be able to survive this all in a balanced and harmonious manner, or will they eventually go the way of the West and Asia's "developing" nations?

Will this vertical graveyard be an omen for the future or remain an unfortunate lesson from the past?

Alas, only time will tell.

Tashilungpo

Where Goddess and Buddha Dwell

Her arid peak, peppered with the green of a few hardy plants, has a power revealed even more fully to the mind than to the eyes.

Five centuries have now passed since Buddhist saints and sages established a monastery on her slopes. And somewhere in the course of its founding they came to comprehend the inherent power of the place.

They determined that the great peak above the future monastic city embodied the energy of the Great Goddess, known as Drolma Jangu, the Green Tara. So they called it Drolmari, Drolma's Peak.

Just now, small groups of pilgrims walk along the *lingkhor*, the circumambulation trail skirting the back wall of Tashilungpo Monastery, which sits megolith-like below her prayer flag-strewn summit.

Drolma is visualized, in some of the pilgrims' minds, as a beautiful green female of perfect body and bearing, surrounded by flowers. She is the divine savioress who looks after all beings through her twenty-one emanations. They possess qualities ranging from the most nurturing to the most "nasty"; each appropriate to some aspect of her mission of succor.

From her eyes and body radiates a clear green light that banishes obstructions to health, happiness and enlightenment for all who closely identify with her through the power of their imaginations.

Meanwhile, inside the monastery's walls, within easy view of the mountainside shrines devoted to Drolma, other divinities are being propitiated for similar purposes.

Among the many buildings and alleyways of this monastic city are *lhakhang*, chapels known as God's Houses, which hold superbly crafted statues, into whose metallic forms the powers of divine beings are imbued through ritual and belief. Among them are sacred spaces known as *dukhang*, chanting and assembly halls where the monks link up with that divine energy outside themselves but, simultaneously, welling up within.

The monastic city of Tashilungpo whose name, Heap of Glory, is most appropriate to its physical form—that of a conglomerate of temples to the enlightened beings embodied in its statues and sacred paintings—is also the residence of the human incarnation of a particularly significant Buddha.

The tantric Buddha of Boundless Light, Öpame, or Amitabha in Sanskrit, holds forth occasionally from Tashilungpo in his flesh and blood "body basis" of the Panchen Lama.

Like Drolma, Öpame too radiates a saving light. His glow is a warm, reddish-orange, like the setting sun in whose domain, in fact, his paradise is said to exist.

He is red, too, like the joyful quality of mind that arises from transforming the restraints of one's physicality and emotional ecology into a clearly perceiving consciousness. He is the primary emblem of this process in the tantric scheme of things.

In a real way, by walking around Tashilungpo, on the three-kilometer-long circumambulation trail under Drolma's Peak, one become bathed in the auras of two of the most benevolent enlightened beings, linking up with these two fundamental forces for enlightenment.

The pilgrims walk a fine line between the two saving energies of Drolma and Öpame, taking on the qualities of each in perfect union.

A Stitch in Time

The sunsetting stillness along the alleyways and courtyards of Tashilungpo Monastery is suddenly shattered by the tattoos of long horns, cymbals and drums.

After a long day of chanting, praying and exercising the joint will of their imaginations, the monks have come to the climax of the four-day ceremony, held on behalf of the health and welfare of their spiritual leader, the Panchen Lama.

As the long procession of the monks and their instruments winds along the monastery's alleyways, the atmosphere becomes increasingly charged with an indefinable energy.

Lay people seem to materialize out of every nook and cranny in the labyrinth of buildings that composes this monastic city. They join the procession on its journey to the ritual ground.

In time, after all the monks are assembled, we onlookers are admitted through a portal into the debating garden. The sizeable crowd surges forward in eager anticipation and forms a thick wall to one side of the broken circle of monks. All breathlessly await the monks to begin the ceremony known as *torgyak*.

Off to one side of the ritual orchestra, a long line of *torma* offerings are arrayed on the ground. They include one large butter and barley flour sculpture covered with death's skulls, and what appear to be real animal entrails. Several smaller *torma* are there as well. All are a somber maroon in color, and wonderfully hideous.

Hideous, that is, to our sensibilities, but so very alluring to sentient obstacles such as ghosts and demons who would cause illness, death or misfortune to befall the ceremony's beneficiary.

By this time, the atmosphere has become exceedingly charged, permeated by a seriousness that can be felt in every fiber. The tattoos from the instruments are now sustained and deliberate. The crowd, hushed. Monks and lamas stand deep in concentration, visualizing the vibrant "inner" forms of these grotesque "outer" objects. Through the power of their imaginations they offer up the essence of the *tormas*—beautiful palaces in the eyes of the obstacles—for the continuing prosperity of the Panchen Lama.

After nearly one half hour of intense mental offerings, punctuated by the mysterious sounds, the dam finally breaks. The offerings are deemed to have been accepted on the subtle mental plane.

Since the outer forms are temporal and impermanent things, having been made for this ceremony alone, the *torma* must now be disposed of in the prescribed manner. As the ceremony is a kind of exorcism, and its objects, rather fierce and dangerous beings, disposal of the *torma* by fire is in order.

The straw pyre is doused liberally with gasoline at the designated spot beyond the northern gate of the garden. Similarly, fires during the previous three days have been set to the other cardinal directions of the "outer" *mandala* which is Tashilungpo *gompa*. And all such immolation places are situated at a crossroads so that the obstacles can disperse easily and quickly.

The area around the pyre is cleared dramatically by baton-wielding monks, while others somewhat hesitatingly carry the large *torma* to its fiery end. As the musical instruments pump away the pyre is ignited; the *torma*, immolated.

The smaller *tormas* are scooped up by onlookers who will repeat the fiery process with them in their own household hearths, so as to protect the family from similar spiritual onslaughts.

Fighting fire with fire is that necessary "stitch in time," Tibetan style.

Phantoms in the Sunlight

Like phantoms they appear. First materializing in one gaily painted doorway then another. Then, two by two. Ultimately, they arise in groups, as if from nowhere: golden phantoms out of the intense Tibetan sunlight and worn stony recesses of Tashilungpo Monastery.

They float along its narrow lanes in huge robes and crescent-shaped hats, both colored gold. They appear, from the distance, like Hawaiian kings in procession or troops of Alexander the Great on the march.

Whatever the origin of their huge caps and capes, the monks of Tashilungpo evoke an exceedingly ancient image in an equally ancient place.

The crowd of golden phantoms grows, as do their good-natured inquiries of this phantom, coming from a place as unfathomable to them as is theirs to me. "What is your name?" "Where are you from?" "How long will you remain here?" "Where did you learn our language?" come the rapid-fire questions.

The mood is almost one of gaiety as the huge crowd of sunlit phantoms proceeds onto the main chanting hall of this vast monastic city. It carries me along, like the flotsam and jetsam in a powerful tide.

After negotiating narrow, dimly lit passageways and smooth stone steps, we find ourselves in the open air courtyard of the Tsokchen Dukhang, housing the chanting hall and scores of shrines. The monks are now congealing like a frenzied swarm of Yellow Jacket hornets. They buzz deafeningly as they intone an initial chant of invocation.

Suddenly, as if a single organism of one mind—much like a hive of bees—they burst from the porticos surrounding the courtyard into the main chanting hall, to buzz even more intensely during a ceremonial offering of *tsog*, the food of Buddhist communion.

The suddenness of the onset of the monks; the bright golden color of their caps and robes; the intensity of their presence; and the abruptness of their entry into the glowing, statue- and silk-adorned chanting hall has been a thrilling experience.

Such is always the case, in close encounters with phantoms of a sunlit kind.

A Bright Darkness

The Tantric God's House is bathed in a bright darkness.

Dark as the depths of the soul: the obscure world into which the chanting monks delve by means of ceremonies invoking the most active qualities of their own consciousnesses.

Dark as its well-worn altars enshrining images of various *yidams*, tantric tutelary deities, some quite dark and fierce in demeanor. Their faces are covered in silk shrouds to mask them from uninitiated eyes that strain to see it all: butterlamp lit woodwork, carpets, paintings, statues, elaborate ritual implements and musical instruments.

Dark as for dreaming then harnessing, in waking, the powers of our imaginations.

Dark as the habitual state of our minds.

Dark as the depths of the Tantric God's House at Tashilungpo Monastery.

But bright.

A brightness recognizing the potential rainbow-colored, clear light inherent in all of our minds.

Brightness in the availability of techniques to unlock that light which dispels the dark things of our souls and eventually shines through into our conscious awarenesses.

Bright light pulsates below it all.

It's like the vivacious bells, drums, horns and chants of these tantric monks.

Like the images of deities materializing three dimensionally to them, through the powers of their imaginations and discipline of their practices.

Like that great leap in mind allowing them to finally see out from their tutelary buddhas' eyes.

A bright darkness.

Sakya

Spirit of the Gray Earth

It has grown out of the gray earth and for centuries has been enriched by it. And, in its turn, has nourished the spirits of the people in its isolated valley.

Like a mushroom that appears magically out of the barren soil, Sakya *gompa*, the Solitary Place of the Gray Earth, is totally at one with its austere and arid valley. It is of the essence of this spot of Tibetan land.

Almost every building that one sees in the Tibetan countryside—even today—is made from solid, native rock. Here people build for utility, rarely for vanity. Buildings are not made only for the presently living but for generations of beings yet to come.

Tibet is timeless, an eternal place. Sakya Monastery, like the valleyscape which it dominates with an unshakeable inertia, too is eternal.

It is eternal in the sense of human time, having occupied this site for almost one thousand years.

It is eternal, too, in the sense of the message it brings to an unhappy world outside and below its strangely beautiful valley. A message describing a universe teeming with splendidly beauteous and horrendously exciting divinities; of sights and sounds which, in the end, are the self-same energies coursing through each of our minds.

As one shuffles through its richly painted and decorated halls, past statues of ancient teachers, saints and divinities, past its huge tree trunk pillars and gray and red-stained stone walls, one begins to sense the gravity of its message.

One begins to understand that stability of purpose and quality of centeredness which Tibetans have continued to draw upon, despite the cyclonic winds of ignorance and terror that have been blowing over its peaks and valleys for more than a generation now.

Like the massive landscape of which it is an inextricable expression—like that inexpressible landscape within—Sakya *gompa* stands solidly for the spirit of all our home places, be they out in the "natural" world, or within.

"Home is where the heart is," so they say. Sakya *gompa* is a home to the spirit in the heart of the Altar of the Earth.

INTO THE HIGHLANDS
THE SNOW PEAKS AND BEYOND

"To describe the eastern ocean's mountains
would require a very long tale;
the white rocky mountains are palaces of snow lions
and the lower slopes are *mandalas*.
I've a horse like white rock candy
and the saddle, a red rocky eagle;
riding the horse is the great saint Milarepa."
—from an old Tibetan folksong

Land and Spirit

Free Souls in a Free Land

"Where are your menfolk?" we asked.

"Up there, with the yaks," answered the nomad woman, pointing vaguely in the direction of the tundra-clad, eighteen thousand foot high "hills."

Good fortune had brought us to a nomad encampment in the shadow of Gyatso-la, the highest pass between Lhasa and the high Himalayas, their timeless abodes.

Theirs was a tiny encampment consisting of three woven yak hair tents; two massive, growling watchdogs; a loom for weaving woolen panels to be sewn into *chuba* cloaks and colorful aprons; piles of animal dung being dried for fuel; and assorted other necessities for living the nomadic lifestyle.

At last, here were some of those free souls living the age-old, transhumant lifestyle in the highlands, amid golden-colored tundra and the watery floodplain of a huge graveled river.

They call themselves *drokpa*, "people of the uncultivated lands." They are, in their perennial lifestyle, a foundation of the Tibetan way of life. And their tent, the Tibetan "Home Sweet Home."

One need only look around in any Tibetan town, especially

during the warmer months, to realize the Tibetans' nomadic roots. Tents seem to pop up everywhere—not, of course, the dark brown, woven yak hair variety, but white cotton ones, gaily designed with appliqué panels of auspicious symbols and sacred animals. For when the week's work is done, out come the tents, carpets, food and *chang* beer for large picnic-style encampments.

During the rest of the week, one can usually find sunshade canopies draped partially over the courtyards of Tibetan homes, made much like the panels of tents. Cotton on the one hand, adobe and stone on the other, they are people, even when settled, who have not forgotten their nomadic roots.

Tibetans' roots go far back in time in a timeless land, where the essence of their rootedness lies in their rootlessness. As such the nomads are preservers of that which is uniquely Tibetan.

For us equally rootless, but much less firmly rooted Westerners, the nomads have a particularly valuable message. They tell us that having a sense of rootedness does not come from being fixed in the concrete of cities and rigid beliefs, but reveling in the unshackled freedom of the uncultivated elements and their associated states of mind.

The Colored Earth

Streaks of rocky red, alternating with serpentine green, and crowned with yellow grasses that are more tundra than meadow have replaced the lusher valleys, now but a verdant memory below us.

We've entered the zone of color atop the Altar of the Earth.

A realm where variegated mineral distillates of the blood and body of Mother Earth hold sway.

A place of rocks in all sizes and shapes. Of graveled rivers and the rare bird flicking from one tawny outcrop to the next.

A land in which even the hardiest of the hardy Tibetan people think twice about living. It is the arid boundary between the realm of the people—spreading distantly below us—and the snow-capped realm of the gods, beginning to loom up out there, above us.

All is austerely beautiful in this arid palette of earthy pastels.

Earlier on, in the more hospitable valleys, one noticed everywhere the touch—albeit, generally a light and respectful one—of the human hand: adobe and stone villages seeming to grow right out of the earth; checkerboard fields of barley, wheat, rape seed and vegetables; sheep, goats and cattle roaming among it all. And, atop adjacent mountains and hills, innumerable prayer flag-adorned shrines to earth divinities. But one also saw the forlorn ruins of monasteries and fortresses shorn from their high perches by an angry political hand.

Up here, the presence of humanity is easily forgotten as one looks outward, toward the greatest works of the physical world. The snow covered peaks testify to the inexorable tectonic surges that formed these great mountains and rivers so recently, after the collision of Island India and the Asian landmass.

These austere expressions of the forces of nature affect one now—as they must the Tibetans—in an overwhelmingly mystical manner.

They are beyond being mountains and deeply cut valleys; more than snow, ice and tundra. They are metaphors to the upward surge of one's spirit; earth-colored beacons to the soul on its search for perfection; sunlit models of enlightenment.

This Wild Land

Tibetans say that their ancestress was a denizen of the rocky crags—the Great Goddess in an ogress' form. It is absolutely understandable in this context along a wild stretch of road. The rocky land only begrudgingly yields to this sole artery, linking Lhasa with its sister cities of Gyangtse and Shigatse, way to the east of here.

One must indeed be part rock goddess to call this wild land one's home. One sees her descendants living along furiously churning rivers, circulatory channels fed by great glaciers, atop mountains that tower over their fourteen-thousand-foot high valleys.

One finds them in mud and stone houses looking more like the wild outside environment than human-made shelters. The earthy villages are so fully blended with the environment that one knows they are there only by the green and yellow planted fields and the rainbows of prayer flags fluttering from the four corners of their rooftops. Only then does one notice the earthen dwelling camouflaged among the pastel-hued mountains.

In all respects they live woven inextricably into the warp of this wild land and the woof of the great forces of the weather which shapes it.

Whereas farmers in other parts of the world wrench heavily at the earth with steel plows, chemicals and "scientific" methods in order to win illusory surpluses and profits from its substance, Tibetans touch it lightly—for survival's sake—and with reverence.

They know, in the long run, that they are at the whim and mercy of the earth and weather, as are we all. They know that its essence (we call it molecules) is one and the same with that which courses through their veins.

From this unspoken awareness comes reverence. From it comes the sure knowledge that the hills and rivers are alive—not just with animals and plants—but with a kind of transcendant sentience with which they are embraced in an everlasting dance of life. And death.

So Tibetans hang out prayer flags at mountain passes, at precipitous river banks, at shrines to divinities of the land and atop their own roofs, to signal reverence for the noumenal energy inherent in it all.

Likewise, they burn quantities of *sang*, juniper incense, in braziers large and small, each morning and on ceremonial occasions. These are meant to please the full range of divinities: buddhas, and gods of the earth and water who compose the sentience of all landscapes, within and without.

In every way, and at all times, Tibetans consciously strive toward a firm footing in this wild land of form and spirit.

Altars of the Earth

As far as the eyes can see, snow and ice.

The great earth altars spread precipitously in practically every direction about Lakpa-la pass. They glisten significantly in the intense sunlight, as they jut upwards of twenty-three thousand feet into the stratosphere.

Their names are well known as targets of mountaineers: Shishapangma, Dorje Lakpa, Tseringma-Gauri Shankhar and Melungtse, among others. But to the natives on both slopes of their rocky spine they are abodes of the greatest divinities of the earth.

For Tibetans, their spiritual powers pervade every aspect of life below their sacred summits. No wonder a philosophy as infinite as Buddhism found a willing audience among these rugged highland people.

Models such as the great peaks give wings to the spirit; allow it to speculate and find comprehension in the infinite Buddha Mind, that flux which is said to permeate all phenomenal reality like rays of rainbow-colored light. So, it's not hard to imagine how these brightly lit massifs, sticking up into the realm of rainbows, have become potent metaphors for the attainment of enlightenment.

Just imbibe of the scene. The jagged peaks and massive white glaciers against a deep blue sky, the profound tawny-colored canyons and turquoise rivers; they are the playing fields of snow lions and *yetis*.

Imagine too, golden thrones, glistening within rainbow-lit temple-palaces of archaic deities at their summits. Some of the highest of the Himalayan peaks are dedicated to goddesses called the *Tsering Chenga*, the Five Great Long Life Sisters. The great mountain, Gauri Shankhar—known to Tibetans as Tseringma—is the base of the abode of Tashi Tseringma, leader of the sister goddesses who are aboriginal protectors of this land, its people and their spirituality. She and her four sisters were, much later, enlisted into the service of Buddhism by Milarepa, the illustrious eleventh-century Tibetan saint who had sought enlightenment in caves below their peaks.

Tashi Tseringma is the epitome of beauty, with her stunning white face, rich clothing and many jewels. And one of her sisters is well known to rest of the world through the mountain on which she dwells. She is Meyalungsangma, the divine bearer of food and wealth, but is better known by her honorific title of Chömolungma, Mother Goddess of the Land, the name given by the local people to Mount Everest.

Taken together, the Himalayas are a great barrier reef in the ocean of air. They keep the steaming lowlands from obscuring the pristine clarity of this highest plateau on earth. And, simultaneously, they preserve the highest teachings on the nature of reality for the benefit of that same world below it, whether or not it can yet appreciate this legacy.

The awe-inspiring vista renews one's being and reinforces one's faith in the possibilities of living. The great peaks are Guideposts to the Spirit; Pillars of the Sky; Altars of the Earth.

The Gates of Heaven and Hell

The dusty road narrows considerably as it begins its undulating passage off the Tibetan Plateau. It twists alongside the churning river and eventually descends through the chasm which Nepali traders in olden days used to call the Gates of Hell.

The shrubs and junipers of this strangely beautiful plateau—one of the world's great deserts—linger still in the rocky scree along the chasm's great escarpments, despite intermittent forays by the lowland's mists. Yet even here, amid great snow peaks and profound canyons, the insinuating wetness has begun to change the entire face of things.

Here, on the receiving end, the uplifted folds of granite show the telltale green stubble of lowland species, something rarely seen on the Plateau, outside of Tibet's irrigated valleys. They gain a foothold on those slopes that are repeatedly hit by moist breaths from the Indian Ocean and form a salt and pepper array of yellows to sherwood green, set off by autumnal reds.

Already the air has changed from the light sharp odorless currents one smells (or ''not smells'') atop the Altar of the Earth, to the damper, rather aromatic principle that one had forgotten ever existed.

Before one's very eyes, the oceanic mists gather more and more fully, often blocking out whole forests that cling to granite canyon walls.

This is the crack between the worlds of high and low; hard and soft; difficult and facile; sacred and profane.

All unfolds like an incredibly vivid, widescreen color movie replete with intense smells and feels as well as the obligatory sights and sounds.

Descending into the canyon the mists and chill increase exponentially as the river makes itself ever more strongly felt.

Suddenly, meadows! Real meadows, of wildflowers, herbs and berries; meadows of variegated greens, purples, yellows and reds, cut by streams furiously rushing past moss-clothed boulders and banks of shaggy grasses.

The plants grow in a furious tempest here, just as the lowlands are populated by so many colors, descriptions and shapes of humanity.

A meadow such as this is a dazzling cornucopia to any eyes. But to those now accustomed to the subtle color shifts and forms of the Tibetan Plateau, it is like returning to Earth from Mars.

No rest for the senses. The scene keeps shifting dramatically as we descend through dense forests, fierce cataracts, turbulent mists, thick groves of ferns and moss, water dripping everywhere.

A better name for this place (the dangerous road notwithstanding) must be the Gates of Heaven.

Like land, like people. The Tibetan highland folk are like their land: direct, primal, hardy and mystical. Down under, in the Kathmandu Valley and beyond, people too are exceptional but they already live in another ecozone, in both a physical and mental sense. They are part of that bewilderingly complex lowland world that has, for millennia, given rise to great material and spiritual achievements but also to plagues, wars and enforced ignorance.

Until the tragic era that began a generation ago, Tibetans were, by dint of their highland fastness, relatively safe from the pendular swings and vicissitudes of our flatland mentality. Of course, all that has now radically changed. Still one can suspend time amid these profound canyons, and with the powers of the imagination send a little bit of heart and mind back up there, to that special world and reality beyond the Gates of Heaven and Hell.

Song of Tibet

Mountains so steeply,
taking my breath away,
pierce the sunny sky;
like great white sheep,
clouds herded gently,
slowly carry me away.

Sands shifting smoothly,
dreaming time away,
heat shimmers in the sky;
all move so slowly,
noisy thoughts ceasingly,
quietly carry me away.

Rivers so freely,
wending their mighty way,
in canyons of earth and sky;
transparent feelings,
reflecting clearly,
dissolve and carry me away.